NASCAR NATION

CHRIS MYERS

WITH MICHAEL LEVIN

NASCAR NATION

HOW RACING'S VALUES
MIRROR THE NATION'S

FENN
M&S

NASCAR

Myers, Chris
  NASCAR nation / Chris Myers.

ISBN 978-0-7710-6118-9

  1. NASCAR (Association).
2. Stock car racing--United States. I. Title.

GV1029.9.S74M93 2012   796.720973   C2012-900970-9

We acknowledge the financial support of the Government of Canada through the Canada Book Fund and that of the Government of Ontario through the Ontario Media Development Corporation's Ontario Book Initiative. We further acknowledge the support of the Canada Council for the Arts and the Ontario Arts Council for our publishing program.

Published simultaneously in the United States of America by Fenn/McClelland & Stewart, a division of Random House of Canada Limited, P.O. Box 1030, Plattsburgh, New York 12901

Library of Congress Control Number: 2012932350

Printed and bound in the United States of America

Fenn/McClelland & Stewart, a division of
Random House of Canada Limited
One Toronto Street
Suite 300
Toronto, Ontario
M5C 2V6
www.mcclelland.com

1   2   3   4   5   16   15   14   13   12

The opinions expressed in this book are those of the author and do not directly represent NASCAR.

All photos courtesy of Getty Images except as noted.

CONTENTS

IN LOVING MEMORY OF MY SON,
CHRISTOPHER MYERS,
AND MY FATHER, EUGENE T. MYERS.

1

STRAPPING IN

'll never forget the first time I heard the national anthem played at a NASCAR event after 9/11. It was the first race after the tragic fall of the twin towers in New York. The audience was enormous. There was a real sense of community, a sense of togetherness unlike any race I had been to before.

What happened next is difficult to explain. There was no preparation for it. The crowd just started chanting "U.S.A." in unison. It didn't start with a single voice. Just as everyone stood up together, they started chanting together: "U.S.A." They were reciting more than three letters. They were chanting for the United States of America and everything it stood for, all of its values, and they were saying it in unison. They weren't saying it in an abrasive or in-your-face kind of way. They were saying, "We are Americans, and we will stay together."

That's NASCAR – as American as baseball and apple pie, and it embodies all of the values that make America great. It's cars and crashes, but it's also a multi-million dollar American tradition born out of a grassroots southern racing sport. NASCAR may have started small as an underdog in sports, but it has grown to international acclaim. That's the great American story – the unexpected rise to success.

NASCAR could have only started here, in a country where learning to drive is as essential as learning to walk. The automobile is inextricably a symbol of America and American industry, and it's a part of most Americans lives. We drive more and unfortunately consume more oil than most other countries. While high oil consumption isn't the goal, when we ask, "What is America?" the answer always seems to be that it is the land of opportunity. It's the open road.

NASCAR is all about the open road with no speed limit and no stop signs, with things coming at you faster than you know how to handle them. Drivers have to expect the unexpected and possess lightning-fast reflexes. Most Americans can relate to the need for speed, the call of the open road, and the cross-country adventure. The car has been part of the American dialogue since Henry Ford.

If cars are for most Americans, then NASCAR is also for most Americans. Baseball is America's pastime and football is America's passion, but NASCAR is its roots. Fans don't have to pay thousands for seats to see a race. Families come down in campers, kids and all, for the weekend of a big race. It's family time and it's NASCAR time. That's why NASCAR has such a sizeable and loyal fan base. I am but one steadfast fan out of millions.

NASCAR is a major part of America, and now, a part of who I am. However, it wasn't always easy getting into the sport. Before I started broadcasting for NASCAR, I was a so-called stick-and-ball guy. I had no idea what that meant, but I heard it a lot during my early days. I thought I was a sportsman and broadcaster, but as I got into the world of race cars, even as a major professional sports broadcaster, I learned that NASCAR was a world in and of itself.

During my ten years at ESPN, I had covered a little bit of racing. I'd interviewed some of the legends in the sport: Jeff Gordon and Dale Jarrett, who won the Daytona 500 (in fact he won the race three times – 1993, 1996, and 2000 – and his father was also in the sport). When I was with FOX and they acquired the broadcast rights to NASCAR, they were looking for a host. This is how it all began.

Now, they tried out several different people, and each and every job candidate was impressive and overwhelmingly qualified – I was definitely not a shoe-in. They knew they wanted to bring in Darrell Waltrip, the former NASCAR champion. They were looking at former NASCAR crew chief Jeff Hammond. Of course there was Larry McReynolds, the longtime NASCAR crew chief and sports analyst. These guys might have had limited broadcasting experience, but if anyone knew racing, it was them. They were NASCAR insiders. FOX tried out a lot of different people who really knew the sport. I was the underdog.

Contrary to what some people believe, NASCAR isn't a game just for the winners. With the way the dollars work out, it's thought that only four to five teams can afford to compete; that it's a game only for those who can pay to compete, shutting out the underdog. While some of this may be true, there are unexpected wins to counter that claim. Take then-rookie Brad Keselowski's steal at Talladega on April 26, 2009. There were four laps to go, and Dale Earnhardt Jr. looked like he might win. Tony Stewart's car didn't seem to be getting up to speed. By the last lap, it was Carl Edwards who held the race in the palm of his hand. No one thought Keselowski was going to take it. Suddenly, Edwards's car, nosed by Keselowski's, somersaulted in the air, destroying the front end of Ryan Newman's car. Edwards exited the car and ran to the finish line on foot after all the cars had already sped across it. Keselowski was in the lead. Luck plays a big role in racing.

And as luck would have it, I ended up getting the job with FOX as an on-air host. One day I was in the building and someone said, "You're a guy who knows broadcasting. You know how to ask all the questions." They said this knowing that I wasn't as knowledgeable about the sport as the other candidates. I told them that I could study any sport, and besides – I'd grown up around racing. So I was given an opportunity to take a job that would change my life: I became the host of the NASCAR pre-race show.

As a broadcaster, I was expected to make sure that I was both sufficiently informed and connected to the audience – and boy, do you get an audience. I took the responsibility seriously from the very beginning. NASCAR is one of the greatest sports in the United States and has one of the most dedicated fan bases. Becoming a NASCAR broadcaster was no simple task. I had the job, but I still had to figure out how to become a part of the NASCAR world. Unlike many other sports, NASCAR wasn't just about giving stats on air. I had to take a lighter approach, because people want to be entertained. They want to enjoy themselves; it's a fun and down-to-earth sport. People watching the race aren't watching it just to hear numbers. If I wanted to do this, I had to really become a part of the NASCAR world – which is easier said than done.

"Hey, there's Chris Myers," the late David Poole, a writer for the *Charlotte Observer*, said as he stood with a beer in hand after a race. "I thought when you came on NASCAR you would suck." Believe it or not, Poole was trying to bring me into the tight-knit NASCAR community with his frank comment. He went on to say, "But I was wrong. You're really good."

It turned out that Poole had his own radio show and was a NASCAR insider. As I got to know the people, he was one of those in the NASCAR circle who let me in. He and the drivers themselves were very cooperative and helpful. David always seemed to be saying, "You know we want you – you're a guy we've seen who has worked in the sports world and you're part of this." Poole, his beer, and his welcoming demeanor were my way into a club of sorts; one that you have to respect and want to be a part of. It has core American values – sincerity and honesty – and it values people who are down-to-earth and true to themselves. When I went down to Daytona, the drivers walked me through the garage so I could see how things worked. It was their way of including me in the game.

Here's the thing about NASCAR: it's an all-American, traditional sport that stays true to its roots, while it's also modern and cutting edge. The social aspect has changed little. The old NASCAR was a southern regional sport. So for a new broadcaster, there were times I felt as if it were saying, in a southern drawl: "You're not one of us." Still, NASCAR has developed with time, welcoming drivers from California, Las Vegas, and every nook and cranny of the U.S.A. What got me accepted in NASCAR was sincerity. As I said, this is a down-to-earth sport, and being honest is an all-American NASCAR value. I didn't try to pretend to be someone I wasn't. I didn't come on like I was Mr. NASCAR. They knew I knew TV, and they gave me a chance to succeed. NASCAR reminded me of a very simple American value: they'll respect you if you're real and sincere.

As a matter of fact, even FOX was put under scrutiny. The network was seen as crazy untraditional television, and somehow insincere. In the end, FOX was able to prove that though it was going to do things differently, the network would be doing them better. It was the first to put the ticker-style running order up on the screen for the race. That's only one example of the many technical things that our production and broadcast crews have contributed to the sport, getting fans at home closer to the races.

In truth, I'm only a small part of it all. The true honor goes to those behind the scenes who are rarely mentioned. In NASCAR, everyone matters, and every member of the crew is essential to both the races and the on-air production. It's because of each of us that our broadcasting team is the most popular among NASCAR fans and has been broadcasting for over eight years. We have a nice mix of people, and we can cover the news stories right, relate to drivers, and have fun. That's what people want to see. Not only that, but our FOX team has now been credited for making the sport more mainstream and being cutting edge on air.

As much as being a broadcaster and a member of an amazing crew has allowed me to be an active part of the sport, I also consider myself a fan, in the stands, cheering "U.S.A." with everyone else. I'm just as amazed, fascinated, and perplexed by the sport as the rest of the onlookers. My eyes are always wide open, catching every moment, no matter how many races I see. The bright colors of the cars speeding around the gargantuan tracks never lose their shine – the frenetic flags flapping in the air, cars shattering like glass. However, it's more than visual; all of the senses are affected. The clouds of smoke, the smell of the fumes, the size of the mammoth track and the scent of the rubber, fuel and oil after a wreck, the sounds of cars zooming by – you definitely need earplugs.

And the experience isn't only reserved for people in the stands. NASCAR is one of the great TV sports because fans can experience it in a way that they just can't with other sports. The drivers let us put microphones and cameras in the cars; we can listen in on the radio communication between the drivers and their crew chiefs. This adds an entirely new element to the race that isn't possible in other sports. Imagine being able to hear a football player talk to his coach as he makes an important pass or being able to talk to a baseball player as he runs from home plate to first base. Well, we can talk to drivers at every moment. In the middle of the race, if a driver's car wrecks, he's able to talk to you to explain what happened. Fans can't get that close to the action and certainly not to the players themselves in football or baseball. But in NASCAR, fans can walk into the pit-road area before the race and stand, as if in some shrine, in front of the same cars that they see on the track a couple hours later.

But NASCAR is more than just cars. There's an important human element to the race. For every lap of a NASCAR race, a driver has to make countless split-second decisions: how to start; whether to overtake the car in front or to "draft" (hang behind the car in front, reducing air resistance); when to gain or maintain speed; where and when to turn, brake, or gas; how to dodge crashes; and whether to change that tire that may be in need of a change or to stick it out (hoping it won't cause a crash or a blow-out that will cost the race). Every track is unique, calling for different driving techniques on the part of the driver and putting new demands on the car and the crew. It's driving at its fullest – a sport most Americans participate in every day in their own vehicles. It's something everyone can relate to, but here cars are moving faster than 180 miles per hour for exceptionally close finishes and lawsuit-and-insurance-penalty-free car crashes.

At the beginning, I was most interested in the human element of the sport. As someone who had interviewed football and baseball players for years, I was fascinated less by the cars and more by the drivers. It isn't just about making the play, but what the players are thinking about while doing it. Their teammates, the plays, the coach, their family in the stands – all of these elements actually play a major part in the psychology of the player and thus also play a major part in the outcome of the game.

I had enjoyed witnessing the psychological element in other sports but, when it came to NASCAR, I still wasn't sure if it was about the car that's being driven or the person driving it. The conclusion I've come to now is: it's both. Trying to separate the two is like trying to separate NASCAR from the U.S.A. and the U.S.A. from NASCAR. I quickly learned when I started broadcasting that the sport was a lot more than finely engineered cars.

The race revealed itself to me to be a test of intelligence, both on the part of the driver and the crew working behind him – the crew members who keep the car in top racing condition, changing tires and refueling at record speeds. Everything happens so fast, people have to be on their toes. That's why the sport is so popular: people simply like speed, and they like cars, no matter who's driving them or who's winning.

Danica Patrick has become only the third woman to run in the Daytona 500, after Shawna Robinson (1995) and Janet Guthrie (1977), who ran the race twice. Patrick didn't get into a NASCAR ride just because she's an attractive woman. She's achieved six top-ten finishes at the Indy 500 and has proven herself as a capable driver. There's certainly pressure on her to stick in NASCAR and win races. Although she didn't grow up racing go-karts like many NASCAR drivers, she is competing at the NASCAR Nationwide Series level to earn her spurs and a NASCAR Sprint Cup ride. You've also got to trust Tony Stewart's judgment – he believes that she's worthy of a ride, so she'll have every opportunity to prove herself. It was announced that in 2012, Patrick will be driving for Stewart-Haas Racing, a NASCAR team owned by Tony Stewart and Gene Haas.

Not all open-wheel (single seat cars with wheels outside the car's body) racers have come to NASCAR and found success. For example, drivers Patrick Carpentier and Dario Franchitti were unable to replicate their open-wheel track records in NASCAR. The betting is that Patrick will find a way to win.

In the past five to ten years, drivers' profiles have changed and gotten younger. They used to be mature, married men. Today, NASCAR driving isn't only for those drivers, but it's not just for the young athletes, either – it's everybody's sport. And whether people want to call them athletes or not (and I think they are because of what they do and the way that they do it), their driving skills and the decisions that they have to make are a true measure of mental dexterity. What matters in NASCAR, more than any other muscle, is the mind.

Some critics of the sport ask, "If drivers are so intelligent, why do they risk their lives driving in circles, crashing their cars into walls?" They view the admiration of a wreck as grotesque. These are people who don't understand the races and who haven't given it an honest chance. The sights, sounds, smells of the wrecks are a necessary part of the spectacle. Perhaps it's the knowledge that these cars have been handmade by some of the greatest engineers in the country and handled by some of the most skilled crews. Or perhaps it's the assurance that the driver is going to step out of the car and be okay. These drivers may crash and total cars, but at the end of the day, they walk away.

There's nothing wrong with a crash, especially in today's races when the necessary safety precautions have been taken to ensure that drivers are guaranteed as much safety as possible. And there's a reason for these precautions. When Dale Earnhardt, who was the face of the sport, died on February 18, 2001, as a result of injuries from a wreck, it changed the world of NASCAR forever.

My introduction to NASCAR as a broadcaster was earth-shattering. Everyone was affected that day – the parents and kids sitting at home enjoying the final lap of the Daytona 500, the drivers who were well across the finish line before they realized what had happened, my fellow broadcasters and I. All of us, as a nation and community, held our breath as car No. 3 stopped moving. Nobody could be sure of what had happened. We hoped, but in vain. Earnhardt and his No. 3 swerved and crashed on the very last lap. Just moments before, everything had been different. Fans at home were holding onto the edges of their sofas, people were standing up in the stadium with joyful anticipation, and we were narrating the final lap of the race with extra tension in our voices – only to be interrupted by speechlessness.

Everyone was waiting, no longer interested in how the end of the race would turn out; waiting to see if Earnhardt would emerge, just like all the other drivers had in most crashes. He was the symbol of NASCAR. His kind gestures, formidable grasp, bushy moustache, and down-to-earth demeanor fully embodied what NASCAR was and is.

After the first man to approach the window became frantic, everything became unsure. This was no ordinary crash. Then ambulances arrived – the only vehicles you *never* want to see racing out onto the track. It was something that no one expected. In the sport where viewers, fans, and drivers learn to expect the unexpected, this was something for which no one was prepared. No matter how many times the race footage was replayed, it never ceased to seem somehow unreal.

Since Earnhardt's death, safety regulations have greatly increased. Some have complained that these safety regulations have caused uniformity in car design. This is possible, but there's no doubt that being sure that these drivers make their way back to their families at the end of the day is vitally important to NASCAR and its fans. It's a family sport – good, safe fun. After this tragedy, many more drivers have been able to drive safely doing the sport that Earnhardt loved, that the nation continues to loves, and that I love, too.

That day brought the end to the career of one of the greatest NASCAR drivers to ever set wheels on a track. It also marked the beginning of my career as a NASCAR broadcaster, and taught me an early lesson: this sport is all about surprises. In the years since, I've learned a thing or two about what makes NASCAR great, and how all the elements of racing – risk, patriotism, teamwork, tradition, and endurance, just to name a few – come together to make this the true American sport. It's not just that we all love fast cars or the thrill of the open road. It's that the values of NASCAR mirror the values of our great nation, the place we call home.

NASCAR fans don't get half the respect they deserve. As a broadcaster, I get an earful from people who are constantly trying to criticize them and put them down. But in all honesty, the values of NASCAR fans really are the values that make America great. That's why fans deserve to be celebrated, not cut down – they're the people who form the backbone of our nation. NASCAR fans aren't backwoods rednecks: they're the quintessential American heroes.

NASCAR is America. And if you love them both: read on.

2

R I S K

NASCAR drivers are confident – they have to be. They think they can overcome anything, and oftentimes, they're right. People who love NASCAR are confident enough to push the envelope to the very edge. It's not about wanting to get hurt or wishing harm on others. The feeling a person gets watching a race is the same feeling they get watching a horror movie. The monster nears the child, reaching its arms out from under the bed.

Of course you don't want to see a child eaten by a monster, but the tension and the excitement of the film lies in the unknown, in the fear, in the hope of a resolution – in the risk.

In baseball or football, this type of risk doesn't exist to the same degree. If an athlete in one of those sports makes a mistake, it is often viewed as detrimental to the game. In NASCAR, however, it only adds to the thrill. Sure, there are plenty of moments when a football, baseball, or basketball viewer may not know what will happen next or may feel excited or worried, but it doesn't compare to the accidents that make NASCAR so addictive.

Carl Edwards is an example of one such NASCAR adrenaline-addict – and I mean that in the best way possible. For the average person, racing at top speeds and crashing into walls would be enough to get their blood rushing – if not to get their heart stopping. Still, Edwards doesn't stop at the races. He keeps going. In his spare time he flies planes, doing stunts in the air. It takes this particular type of person to appreciate the glory of racing from behind the wheel.

There is no doubt that NASCAR is a sport of risks. Still, there have been many measures taken to ensure that risk and fun do not make safety a casualty in this full-throttle sport. The head-and-neck support (HANS) device is one such innovation that has been made mandatory. It was developed by American Bob

Hubbard and is one of two different neck-support devices that drivers can choose. Made out of Kevlar and carbon fiber, with several liners, a visor, fireproof Nomex lining, a communication earpiece, a foam pad, and light outer lining, the system offers the best protection available.

And yet, there are people, perhaps those who relish memories of the old, down-and-dirty, less-regulated NASCAR days, who say the races have lost some of the risk due to additions such as the HANS. It's hard to believe that something that could save a driver from a lethal fracture at the base of the skull could really interfere with the excitement of the race. If anything, knowing that a driver is carefully prepared in case of an accident should make a fan more able to enjoy the good wholesome fun. Fans watch NASCAR as if it were a real-life action movie; they don't want to see a tragedy on the track.

Drivers can also immediately turn off their engines with the flip of a safety switch. This is another example of how NASCAR's technological advancements are working to make racing about the action, not about accidents. These safety devices and new regulations, which range from checking the size of the spoiler, to weighing the car, to making sure all head and neck supports are in place, perhaps soften the reality of the situation, but in no way do they take the risk out of the sport. Risk is essential to NASCAR – it's a defining quality. You can't have NASCAR without risk.

There are many risks in the sport that fans may not notice. Take, for example, the most basic risk of driving at a high speed. Sure, the cars look like they're moving fast on the screen, but it's all relative. People don't realize that these cars are actually burning rubber, sometimes moving at speeds in excess of 180 miles per hour. At such high speeds, the mere ability to control the vehicle, as well as the driver's responsiveness to other drivers, is at risk. The drivers have to manage a 3,450-pound vehicle while hurtling at top speed. No driver could ever say that there wasn't risk involved.

Many drivers have expressed fear about the sport. It's hard to say what makes them face these risks and it's hard to say what makes us want to watch them face it. We don't want anything bad to happen, but that risk creates the tension that keeps the race interesting. That's what risk is – not knowing what might happen. The safety devices allow a person to enjoy the race with a bit less guilt. We don't feel like we're putting someone's life on the line for the sake of our entertainment. We have the comfort of knowing that they, like a tightrope walker with a net beneath them, will not die for our enjoyment.

However, to say that NASCAR is just entertainment is to ignore what that risk means. That risk is more than just fun. It speaks to something greater. Fans admire drivers and their lives. They want to witness the bright cars speeding down the straightaways. Fans want drivers to win the race for them and feel like winners in the process.

It's similar to Spider-Man, Batman, Superman, and all the superheroes in colorful costumes who face life-threatening danger and succeed. Drivers, dressed in full uniform, with their suits on and their helmets over their faces, become superheroes to a lot of fans. They even *look* like superheroes. We don't want our superheroes to lose, but we do want them to fight villains. Can you imagine telling the Caped Crusader not to drive the Batmobile too fast? NASCAR is more than simply a taste for danger. It's a desire to conquer a challenge. If the risk wasn't there, then there would be no challenge, and no NASCAR.

What's great about NASCAR drivers is that they are average people in many respects who are somehow superheroes. They range in age from twenty-five to fifty and older. Some of the guys aren't very tall, nor do they have athletic builds – but they're still great drivers. Mark Martin is in his fifties and at the top of his game. These drivers are human and relatable, so their feats on the race track make us feel like we, too, can succeed when we face challenges, even if the outcome is unsure. NASCAR drivers are real-life superheroes. Children idolize them, women admire them, and men are inspired by them.

Many of these superheroes start out on a dirt path made in the backyards behind their family homes. They begin refining their skill early, and through dedication, perseverance, and natural talent, they ultimately begin a rise to fame and success. The very story of the NASCAR driver is that of risk. When beginning the career path of becoming a driver, who can say where it will end and if it will take you to the desired destination? The risk, like the challenges on the track, must be faced in order for NASCAR to continue. Meeting these challenges calls for a very particular type of athlete and person. Think of Edwards jumping out of a wrecked car and then heading home for a relaxing evening of stunt airplane flying. Now that's a real athlete.

I did not believe that NASCAR drivers were athletic when I started covering the sport, but this type of a personality and spirit must be coupled with an agile mind and body. When a competition forces people to refine the human body and mind to its sharpest elements, those people are athletes, and that is a sport. It's true that driving well is more of a skill than a physical undertaking. Nonetheless, if you are more of an athlete, you are going to be a more successful driver.

The drivers face many physical difficulties while driving. The more their bodies can endure, the better they will be able to race. One hindrance is the physical heat and fatigue it causes. Anyone who has driven for a long duration can understand how the activity can be wearing. Imagine driving long distances at top speeds, racing other drivers, covered in gear and a helmet, sweating, making sharp hairpin turns, and trying to focus – all at once.

With the mental and physical risks drivers are asked to take comes a major test of endurance, and that simple fact is not always appreciated enough by the sporting world. This is a highly competitive sport. Even if these athletes are not athletes in the same sense that baseball, football, and soccer players may be considered athletes, they are pushing their bodies. It is a different type of athleticism. It may be more easily compared to marathon running than to other sports. In marathon running, runners must pace themselves so that they can endure long distances. Driving in NASCAR is a test of endurance, but no one is jogging here – it's all happening at lightning-fast speeds. Driving skill, athleticism, critical thinking, split-second reaction times, quick thinking, and sheer fearlessness are required of the most successful drivers. You don't see the drivers running out on the track, but drivers are always being pushed to endure in much the same way as other athletes, and to take risks that aren't required in many other sports.

Many people mistakenly assume that NASCAR is all about the cars. Sure, hundreds of thousands are spent on perfecting vehicles, including hours of testing and fine-tuning, examining every aspect of the vehicle's performance using complicated telemetry data to achieve the ideal tire suspension and steering, and countless other head-spinning procedures that these cars go through to become superior machines built for competition. Despite all this, the sport isn't about cars. Well, maybe it is about cars – but someone has to drive. The best driver, even with a bad car, will make the most out of what he has, whereas the worst driver with the best car won't get very far.

In the United States, we like to think of our country as the land of opportunity. If we're honest with ourselves, we'll quickly realize that not everyone has the same opportunities. Some are dealt bad hands from the very beginning, born into poor, dysfunctional families, sent to bad schools where they can only be expected to hang out with the wrong kids from a very early age. Think of immigrant families looking for a better life or a struggling small-time farmer, working long hours and still not making enough. Still, these are the people who make up America and the great stories of our country. That's why America loves the underdog, because the greatest Americans have been those who have faced a challenge, been dealt a bad hand, taken a risk, and succeeded against all odds.

That's what makes NASCAR great: the challenge, the risk, and that final cross of the finish line.

But how do drivers get across that finish line? Part of the answer is a combination of endurance and careful strategizing. Drivers have to be flexible and fit to sit in a car for four to five hours. Because it demands so much of their mental and physical capacities, it's very difficult for drivers not to get physically worn down after hours and hours of high-speed racing.

As far as strategy is concerned, drivers must pace themselves and drive according to the track they're on. If drivers are at Talladega Superspeedway in Alabama, for example, they have to drive carefully. Driving there makes for tight racing, which means lots of wrecks. The way drivers maneuver around this track is different from how they would handle another track, as Talladega calls for a certain finesse and strategy, not just speed.

Jimmie Johnson is a good example of a driver who's won a variety of different races on a variety of different tracks: everything from short tracks to superspeedways to intermediate tracks to road courses. Getting across the finish line isn't just about how fast you can go; it's about strategizing and planning how to manage the specific risks particular to each track.

The Coca-Cola 600, which is on the Sprint Cup Series schedule, is the longest NASCAR race. At 600 miles long, not only does it test the drivers' skills, the winner is often the one who endures with grace and patience, takes a daring risk at the end, and steals first place. It's important to know when to play it safe and when to take a chance.

The race is long and risk is always tempered by staying power. To return to the marathon analogy, let's look at the format of a race such as the Coca-Cola 600. Because it is the only 600-mile racing event, it requires that drivers pace themselves. They have to focus the entire time, knowing when to pass and when to draft. For the most part, that focus is channeled toward staying ahead of the pack while still saving energy for those last few laps leading up to the final one, when everything counts the most. But if drivers aren't on top of their game during the whole race, they can fall behind, and then at the end, be out of the race. The best drivers know how to pace themselves, but that isn't to say that most of the excitement happens at the end of the race. It is thrilling to watch over 40 stock cars zipping along, each trying to stay ahead of the other and taking calculated risks to keep them at the front of the pack.

The test of endurance applies just as easily to the cars, which are engineered to very high standards and must meet tough demands. Imagine what would become of the average automobile if it had to endure just a dozen laps at those speeds, without the proper pit crew, machinery, and engineering. NASCAR vehicles must be carefully maintained, even during the race, which is why having a good car can make all the difference; fewer pit stops means more time saved. On the other hand, refueling, changing tires, and making running repairs can really help a car and the driver's time. If major repairs aren't needed, a pit crew can be done in less than fourteen seconds; however, it doesn't mean that the driver isn't sacrificing valuable time. If drivers can save even just a few seconds, it can change the entire outcome of a 600-mile race.

Good drivers know their cars. They have to be able to identify problems and make decisions about whether to continue with the race or head to a pit stop. This means that drivers can't just drive fast and burn rubber; they have to be on the ball, as both drivers and mechanics. They have to judge, solely by the feel and sound of the car, with a crew chief talking in their ears, whether that tire really does need changing. Other issues are sometimes only picked up on through intuition. The driver's inner sense and ability to detect mechanical flaws can be a deciding factor in the race. Races have been lost due to flat tires and car malfunctions; leaders have become followers due to a blown-out tire. Drivers and pit crews who are able to carefully time their pit stops according to their car's needs and the demands of the race are the most successful on the track. Drivers need to know when to trust their machines and intuition – when to take risks and when to play it safe.

Pit crews play a major role in all of this. They do what your mechanic probably takes days to do in a matter of seconds – then again, it's a team of trained professionals concentrating on one vehicle. The driver has to drop speed very quickly, like coming off the highway straight into a driveway. And it might as well be a driveway – the driver is given an incredibly small amount of space to pull into.

Pit activity is closely monitored and regulated according to NASCAR rules. A breach of these rules can lead to damaging penalties for the teams. For example, if a driver goes over the maximum pit-road speed, the team can get assessed with a pass-through penalty where the driver will have to visit the pit road on the next lap and drive at the speed limit as precious time slips through their tense fingers.

While all this is happening, there could be dozens of other teams doing the same thing at the same time. In order for pit stops to be successful, their choreography must be flawless. Crew members are handpicked, oftentimes former college athletes, like hockey players or retired pro wrestlers. They leap over walls and race to cars to change oil and tires at record speeds. Every second is priceless.

Pit crews encounter risks as well, facing countless occupational hazards during every race. After being driven at full throttle, the car's tires are hot with friction when it pulls into the stall. The crew has to immediately spring into action. Besides the physical strain that their bodies go through, they have to be worried about possible injuries, which are unlikely because drivers aren't careless. Nevertheless, if they are, the team will be penalized for it. Carelessness can cost a driver the race. Risk in NASCAR isn't synonymous with carelessness. In fact, drivers can't be careless on the track as they weigh each risk against the possible reward in terms of passing, pit strategy, or any other phase of racing. Carelessness can get you, and others, injured. Taking the right risks is the way to victory.

If drivers want to win the race, they need to know when to take risks and why. They have to know when to make the pit stops, what to ask the crew chief, and how to follow up with critical decisions that can make or break a race. It's about consistency, intelligence, and knowing when to gamble. Making a pit stop takes valuable time; however, fresh tires can give drivers the extra speed that not only makes up time, but can get them ahead. If the stop isn't made, they may end up blowing out in the last few laps and sacrificing the race. Tony Stewart offered a classic example of intelligent risk near the end of the race at Kansas Speedway during the 2009 Chase for the NASCAR Sprint Cup when he had two tires changed instead of four, gambling that he'd somehow hold on. He did, and he beat out competitors who changed all four of their tires. It's a small distinction, but for Stewart, it made all the difference.

The best NASCAR teams and drivers are mentally and physically equipped to face unexpected obstacles and take necessary risks. With pit crews of trained mechanics and athletes, sharp-minded and confident drivers with strong critical-thinking skills, experienced crew chiefs, and specially engineered cars, NASCAR is an extraordinary display of coordinated talent under pressure. It all may seem like a lot of work to race at high speeds, but the purpose of racing is more than getting to the finish line. It's a test of talent and of what people are capable of under pressure. It's a show of skill and a story of perseverance, danger, and success. That's why NASCAR drivers are seen as heroes: because they are taking risks in order to push the limits of what we think we're capable.

It isn't only the guys out on the track who have to take risks – the people in charge have to be open to new risks and challenges as well. A few years ago, Toyota offered its sponsorship to NASCAR. Initially, there was great resistance to the automaker among some of the fans. I acknowledge the importance of supporting American businesses; however, NASCAR stood to succeed economically from the venture. The organization realized the potential and took Toyota up on its offer. NASCAR realized that what happens on their race tracks is one of the most important factors for their business. Without solid competition, which is what Toyota was bringing to the table, there was a possibility of losing fan support. Fans build NASCAR, but fans want to see competition; without that, the fan base is lost. This change of mindset is vital for the sport to continue to grow and expand. By staying open to a certain element of risk, NASCAR realized that it could think big without giving up its roots – and secured a major sponsor and car manufacturer along the way.

Whether it's the corporate masterminds or the individual drivers on the track, risk is fundamental to NASCAR. There are times to play it safe, and there are times when taking a risk is good, natural, and necessary. Within the proper boundaries, risk is as big a part of NASCAR as the race cars themselves – and it can make all the difference.

3

PATRIOTISM

The sky was ominous and dark. Everyone was crossing their fingers and hoping the race could make it to the halfway mark. If only the sun would shine, the race could go the way it always went: the bright sky lighting the track as cars glimmered around the circuit hour after hour, until nightfall when drivers raced beneath the lights and the solemn evening sky. We knew that if we could just get to the 300-mile mark, it would be an official race.

It was the Coca-Cola 600, one of NASCAR's crown jewels, but that didn't stop the rain from coming. It did end up being an official race, just barely making it to the halfway mark before the skies opened up. Still, we never got to the 600th mile that day, and we never got to change the tire pressure in the cars so they could race under the bright lights at night. Yet the day wasn't about the rain or even the race. It was Memorial Day weekend, and one of the most memorable parts of the race happened before it even began.

The clock was nearing noon and the sun shone pale in the North Carolina sky. That weekend the national anthem played robustly as American Black Hawk helicopters circled above the Charlotte Motor Speedway. In the wake of 9/11, President George W. Bush had made a peculiar request that NASCAR officials were happy to honor. Despite being hampered by the rain and the tight schedule, it was no inconvenience to stop the race for a moment of silence to honor troops of the past and present.

In the racing world, everything seems to move at 180 miles per hour, but that day, all the cars stopped in their tracks at the given time, tires steaming. When they screeched to a halt, the fans quieted, and the engines fell silent. It was as if someone had pressed a pause button and the world stopped. In a place where nothing is ever still, there was no motion.

Though it was only for a moment, it was a rich one. Everyone gave their respect for their country, their freedom, and the brave men and women who fought for it. Just like many Americans got into the habit of doing after 9/11, Tony Stewart placed a small flag outside the window of his car. He later said how special it was to be a part of that moment. I think everyone else who was in the stands that day would agree.

The NASCAR drivers, fans, and teams have a very close connection to America's troops. A good number of drivers and crews know people in the military and have an immense respect for the armed forces. Jimmie Johnson drove his patriotically decorated No. 48 car (entirely painted in red, white, and blue stars and stripes like the American flag) to recognize all the branches of the military and honor the military backgrounds of his teammates. Like many NASCAR fans and drivers, I also have a deep respect for our country's military and history, for which I thank my father, Eugene Myers.

In World War II, he was stationed on a ship headed to the fateful shores of Normandy. At the time he was only nineteen. He didn't know he would be a father someday, or that he would inspire his children with his service to his country. He only knew that his country was calling him to a higher duty that required his honor, his courage, and his patriotism.

My father willingly gave all those things at Normandy, and lived to tell the story to his kids and grandkids. That's my personal connection to the U.S. military. And I'm not alone. Many fans and drivers alike have personal ties to the armed forces, and even those who don't have unwavering respect for the men and women in uniform. NASCAR is closely connected to not only America and its ideals, but to its sense of national pride. The level of patriotism that I see in NASCAR is unprecedented.

At any American sporting event there is a connection between the people, the players, and our country as we stand for the national anthem. Competitors stand reverently, side by side as Americans, and give thanks for our country. There is always a sense of togetherness, patriotism, and pride in those first moments – that never changes. But at a NASCAR race, that sense of patriotism extends far beyond those first few minutes. After the anthem ends, its values remain deeply rooted in the hearts of drivers and fans. Even if they're just racing on the track, the fact that Johnson will decorate his car to honor our troops or that Stewart will put a flag outside of his window tells viewers and fans that this community honors the country where their great sport was born. You never see a football team decorate their uniform in red, white, and blue to honor the United States, and you never see baseball players attach flags to their bats or balls. There's simply a strong connection in NASCAR to the military, and a strong connection to the patriotic values and pride that keep this country strong.

NASCAR is a tight-knit community that takes its core values seriously, and one of those values is a respect for country and for each other. I've heard drivers refer to a crew member who served in the military. Sometimes I'll see a driver put an airborne division sticker on his car. That sticker will belong to a fan who's attending the race or who is from the area. These are the types of things that you just don't see in other sports. And the patriotism exhibited in NASCAR is sincere. I've seen drivers and crew members spend time with soldiers off-camera, taking the time to show them around the track. I've heard drivers and crew members invite military to their shops during the off-season. The roots that connect the NASCAR community to our country run deep and strong.

It's hard enough to get ten people to listen all at once; sometimes it seems impossible to get just one person to calm down. So when more than 100,000 people stand at the same time for the national anthem, without prompting, to show appreciation for their country, it's clear that they share the same basic respect for the American people and nation. That's true American pride and patriotism. Those fans enjoy hearing about drivers and crew members who have served in the military or who have family in the service. That's something that's important to them, and something they can respect.

A lot of NASCAR fans are hands-on people. They're hard-working Americans, many of whom have served in the military themselves. They are the ones who give their lives and bodies to make this nation great. They are the spouses, brothers, sisters, parents, relatives, and friends of people who risk everything for what they believe in. Even if some of them do not find themselves flying in Black Hawks or running in uniform through the deserts of Iraq, they are working here at home doing what needs to be done in order for this country to function. Without them there would be no America, and without them there would be no NASCAR. They're willing to sacrifice everything for their families and for their country. Those are true NASCAR fans.

Fans are what build NASCAR; indeed, they are the foundation of all sports. Still, there is a mentality that racing fans share which stems from a strong sense of solidarity and connects them to each other, to NASCAR, and to America. They seem to know that they are working together for the greatness of this country. They see America's finest cars and sharpest drivers out on the race track, supported and sponsored by our formidable companies and corporate empires, and it makes them proud. NASCAR fans have more one-on-one access to the stars of their sport than any other sport in the world – no one would disagree with that.

NASCAR fans come from all walks of life: from a poor rural rebel from the South to a rich urban professional from the North. Since the race is on about once a week, usually on the weekends, it appeals to people who have families and other responsibilities to take care of during the week. By the weekend, they can finally sit down for a few hours and enjoy NASCAR's adrenaline rush.

The NASCAR calendar is actually designed to meet that very need, with races scheduled around the lives of working families. The campgrounds that surround the race track are there for the same reason. NASCAR is a family sport. I'm often amazed at the number of young fans. They enjoy watching the cars, especially if they see a logo of something they like, such as M&M's candy. So they root for that car and learn the driver's names. Sometimes they get into it because their parents are into it. Or they'll root for Ford because their father and grandfather only bought Ford cars, like many families who've been attached to particular brands of American-made vehicles for generations. But after that initial spark, there's something about the sound of the engines, the speed, the action, and the technology that keeps them interested and tuned into the race.

In addition to being a sport for American working-class families, NASCAR attracts the scientifically minded engineers – the gearheads and hands-on brainiacs who are interested in figuring out how a team repairs a cylinder problem or what their technical strategies are. The team owners, some of NASCAR's biggest fans, are particularly involved and interested in engineering, cars, and the mechanical side of things. Take Rick Hendrick, for example. He's driven out on the track and worked in the pits, and he is now the proud owner of not only one of the largest automotive chains in the United States, but of one of the most successful NASCAR teams: Hendrick Motorsports. They've won close to two hundred races in the NASCAR Sprint Cup Series and countless other victories in other series. Their automobiles are some of the greatest cars ever to hit the race track and are carefully constructed from beginning to end in North Carolina, deep in NASCAR country. Their drivers, from Jeff Gordon to Jimmie Johnson, are greatly revered. Dale Earnhardt Jr. left his late father's company, Dale Earnhardt Inc. (DEI), to sign with Hendrick Motorsports. In 2012, Kasey Kahne started racing for Hendrick Motorsports. The team is considered to be the New York Yankees of NASCAR, and it all started with Hendrick's fine leadership and commitment to the sport.

Jack Roush, another owner, exemplifies what NASCAR is all about. He walks around the track wearing a hat that he never takes off and is affectionately known on the circuit as "the cat in the hat." There's something endearing about him; he's not just a businessman or a sportsman but someone who has dedicated his life to what he is passionate about: cars. He knows them inside and out. Roush has been engineering and designing parts for motorized vehicles for years, and has worked with Ford and Chrysler. He's now the co-owner and founder of Roush Fenway Racing, as well as the owner of his own engineering firm.

Richard Childress, a former NASCAR driver, owns RCR (Richard Childress Racing), which fields teams in the NASCAR Sprint Cup Series and other NASCAR-sanctioned series. Childress's first race was as a replacement driver in the 1969 Talladega 500. This kick-started his career, and soon he was racing as an independent driver, registering in the top ten for many years. He ended his racing career when he saw the opportunity to pick up Dale Earnhardt and a sponsorship from Wrangler Jeans. They won championships in 1986, 1987, 1990, 1991, 1993, and 1994. Childress began expanding his racing empire from that moment on, until RCR eventually became the first racing team to win all three of NASCAR's national championship series.

There's also Roger Penske, the owner of Penske Racing – the team that took the Daytona 500 in 2008. But his interest in cars and racing goes back a lot farther than that: he's been racing, buying, and selling race cars professionally for his entire life.

The team owners' high level of interest and involvement in the racing world is unmatched by their counterparts in other sports. They are major fans who decided to do something about it. It's these guys, along with hard-working American families, gearheads, and strategically minded NASCAR fans who tune in religiously every week, who make up the NASCAR community.

To an outsider, it may seem like a community formed around cars crashes. When I first got into the game, I wondered what people were looking for. Then one day, I realized: anyone can drive a great car well, but when something goes wrong, the question becomes, how are they going to handle it? The answer makes the mechanical side of NASCAR so fascinating. So I started watching the cars during the pit stops. I listened to the radio conversations between drivers and pit-crew chiefs discussing whether they should keep going, gambling with worn tires and low fuel, or whether they should lose precious seconds to recharge. Before I got into it, I saw cars just going around in circles – so many wrecks, so many wins. But once I paid closer attention, I realized that there really is something for everybody.

Football and many other sports have, in some ways, become corporate America's sports. That isn't to say that they aren't American or that they aren't great. I'll always be a football fan and I'll never waver in my love for baseball. However, professional football games are too expensive for many Americans to attend, and tickets can be really difficult to attain. The ordeal of getting tickets, snagging good seats, and taking the family along for the experience can be too much of an obstacle for many working Americans.

The campgrounds and the cheap seats at the local racing events make it much easier for NASCAR fans to bring their families along with them to experience the sport. A NASCAR event can be turned into a camping weekend and an all-American family excursion. Although ticket prices have gone up (like everything else), they are still low enough that the stands are full of everyday people. In fact, NASCAR Sprint Cup Series races average larger crowds each week throughout the ten-month racing season than the Super Bowl does every year.

If other sports don't enjoy the same size of crowds that NASCAR does, it may be because of ticket prices. NASCAR fans can afford to be fans. The Daytona 500, like the Super Bowl, has its corporate tie-ins, but tickets are a lot easier to get a hold of. If traveling to a major race like Daytona is too much of a hike, a fan can grab a ticket in a small town or city nearby since NASCAR has locations from North Carolina to California. NASCAR makes it very easy for fans to get involved because it knows that it is nothing without the fans. The organization is big on honoring its roots and tries hard to respect the small-town folks who started it all. NASCAR wants to be not only a family sport, but an affordable one.

Another reason NASCAR is America's sport is because of its singular defining aspect, the invention that makes the sport possible: the automobile. The car defines America. The United States, out of all the countries in the world, has the greatest car culture. Most countries rely much more on mass transit than the United States. From Italy to Russia to Japan, public transportation is generally regarded as more efficient, affordable, and accessible than it is in the United States. This is because of our nation's great automobile industry and our love of cars, both of which stem from the sheer size of the country.

Now, some people will argue that improving our public transportation would do a lot for the country, and I agree. It would open up more stable jobs for drivers, conductors, and mechanics; reduce pollution; cut down on the back-breaking cost and hassle of insurance and constant repairs; get people around faster and easier for less; and help the economy during this never-ending energy crisis. All of those things are true.

Yet there is something about the American car. We're holding onto it, like we hold onto our freedom. The car and the sprawling highway represent more than billions of dollars, lost natural resources, and pollution. Those are the negatives, but there are positives, too. For Americans, car keys and the purr of an engine represent economic power and freedom: the ability to go where you want, when you want. You are the driver and you have control. For many Americans, their car is their second home – we spend a large amount of our days commuting, sitting in traffic jams, or picking up the kids from school and all their activities. We vacation in cars, traveling the open roads for hours on end. What is more American than the cross-country road trip?

When it comes down to it, our cars are extensions of us. There's the cautious minivan, the gear-filled SUV, and the no-frills sedan. A red car says something different than one that's a pale tan. The tank-like trucks on the road, jacked up on massive tires make their drivers feel powerful and in control. Our cars are peppered with bumper stickers that advertise our beliefs and affiliations. And let's not forget those American flags flapping outside our windows that confirm national pride.

Then there's the American terrain: the perfect playground for a strong car culture. We've molded our entire country around the car. We have more highways, side roads, and ways to get from A to B than most places in the world. Many of our cities have mass transit, but often these systems are poorly functioning, and smaller towns don't have anything at all. Ours is not a mass-transit culture. We're drivers and leaders – we like our hands to be on the wheel, in control of our own destiny, not dominated by others.

A car also gives us a sense of responsibility. Owning a car means having to take responsibility for all that it entails: insurance, repairs, gas. Besides all that, it's your car and you have to know the way; you have to drive well enough to get where you're going, whether it's around the neighborhood or the racing circuit. Owning a car is a part of the American dream. We don't want to give it up – it's part of the freedom for which we've worked so hard.

I remember when I was growing up how important it was to get a car. To give up your car would be like giving up a part of your life. In other places in the world, that's not the case. It's one of the things that make the United States unique. Being a car culture makes a sport like NASCAR better understood here than it would be in other places where people don't have that type of connection to cars.

Another characteristic that NASCAR shares with the United States is size. If you visit many European or Asian cities, you may find yourself feeling packed in and abnormally big – like a human in a dollhouse. In the United States, we operate a little bit differently. We built this country to suit our mentality. We like our space. We like our backyards big and our roads wide. We like open prairies, expanses of shining sea, clear skies, broad coastlines, and tall, thick redwoods. We like large pieces of steak bigger than our faces and bellies. Our idea of big and other people's idea of big are two totally different things. We're not packed into a tiny space like many other countries.

So we drive our pick-up trucks, SUVs, and minivans to the race track with big campers and big attitudes to match, pulling into the huge campgrounds outside the track. Eighty thousand to more than 150,000 spectators show up in droves ready to take a seat, set up camp, and whip out supplies for a good ol' barbeque before the race. We admire the enormous race circuit and the sheer size of the spectacle that embodies NASCAR. We stand together for the national anthem. We root and holler for our favorite drivers and teams; enjoy our super-sized hot dogs, hamburgers, and beer; and settle in for hours of quality American sports entertainment.

The demographics of NASCAR mirror those of United States. America is not only a large country – it's incredibly diverse. Think of New Orleans, New York, Los Angeles, Denver, Nashville, Charlotte, Chicago, and all the little towns in between. The diversity of our landscape is what makes this country so interesting. Nowadays, NASCAR's fans hail from all over the United States, and that's had an important influence on how the sport has continued to develop.

NASCAR has made an effort to start catering more to its fans' needs. Trying to make itself more available to everyone, it has set up tracks around the country in new regions. Just like the country in which it was founded, it is always moving forward, stretching its boundaries from sea to shining sea.

That's why the France family – the first family of NASCAR, the folks who started it all in the 1940s and the biggest players in the development of the sport – are pushing NASCAR to the next level. They're even going where there aren't as many fans in order to expand NASCAR's fan base. They know that this is a sport that connects Americans – not just certain types of Americans or Americans who can afford to buy the best seats, but *all* Americans. As well, they're taking NASCAR on the road. They want people from all over the world to appreciate NASCAR. It doesn't have to be a sport just for Americans – it can be a sport that appeals to all car lovers and race fanatics. And there's no doubt in my mind that they'll be successful, just as they've been successful for over sixty years. The reason for their success is simple: the values that NASCAR represents are reflected wherever you go in the grand ol' U.S. of A, and soon, we will see them reflected internationally. Proof of NASCAR's international appeal: EURO-RACECAR was designated a NASCAR touring series in 2012.

Sure, NASCAR started out as a grassroots sport in the South, but today with all its technological advancements, it has truly become a pinnacle of engineering advancement and cutting-edge entertainment. Still, it holds onto its roots and all the morals that come with them. That's why country music, which is also very southern in many ways, has often been associated with NASCAR. Just as country music has become more mainstream, allowing itself to be influenced by pop and rock, NASCAR has become more mainstream, opening up to major broadcasters like FOX and welcoming new advancements to improve the quality of its races.

NASCAR and country music share a lot of the same values. Look at the famous country singer Toby Keith who has played for hundreds of U.S. audiences and has even had the honor of performing for and inspiring our troops. He has said some very moving things about patriotism and the lack of it. Whether this was sparked by some critical comments made by the Dixie Chicks about President George W. Bush and the resulting anger that some country-music fans expressed, I can't say for sure. Politics aside, it's important to be proud of who you are and where you come from and to remember what being an American means. If we forget that and fail to respect ourselves and our leaders, then what do we have?

When Keith said that he would never apologize for being patriotic, this is what he was talking about. Democrat or Republican, liberal or conservative, George Bush or Barack Obama, we need to stand behind our country and our leaders together, in the same way that those NASCAR fans stood together after 9/11 – without prompting, in thankfulness, in solidarity, and with pride. Those are the kinds of Americans who fill the stands at NASCAR races. They're the people we should all strive to imitate: hard-working, patriotic, loyal, sincere, and proudly filled with the American values that make both our country and the sport of racing great.

It's no surprise that this mentality and spirit attract major fans from all walks of life. There's also an enormous appeal for other sports leaders to come over to NASCAR. People who have excelled in playing, coaching, and owning in other sports find themselves drawn to the spirit of NASCAR.

There are several examples of this. Take a look at Joe Gibbs, a man who had a very successful career in the National Football League. He was drawn into the world of NASCAR and created his own team: Joe Gibbs Racing. He hasn't done too badly for himself, either, since switching to NASCAR. He's employed the likes of Tony Stewart and Bobby Labonte, and has taken home three NASCAR Sprint Cup championship trophies. He was apparently retired for some time – I suppose he defines retirement differently than the rest of us, since he came out of "retirement" to go back to work for the Washington Redskins. From Daytona to the Super Bowl, Gibbs has really played the field in the sports world. No great sports enthusiast can stay away from NASCAR for long.

John Henry is another example. Henry is a fascinating person and a fine example of the American dream. His parents were farmers and now he is a trading advisor, owner of the Red Sox, founder of John W. Henry and Company, and co-owner of Roush Fenway Racing.

Both Henry and Gibbs are intelligent businessmen and savvy sports enthusiasts. They're attracted to NASCAR not only for its worth as a sport, but also as a business venture. They know how loyal the fans are, and they know that NASCAR is constantly growing and spreading in popularity while it advances as a sport. They're probably attracted to the sport for the same reason many fans and drivers are: the challenge of a good competition and the ongoing battle of man and machine.

Gibbs won three NASCAR Sprint Cup championships, two NASCAR Nationwide Series owner championships in 2008 and 2009, and a

NASCAR Nationwide Series driver championship in 2009. He once told me that he always wanted to be Richard Petty, not famous football coach Vince Lombardi. Petty was the king of NASCAR, a multi-championship winner, victor of two hundred races, and second-generation driver who lived a fast youth. Yet Gibb's life path seemed to go in another direction. He said his football-coaching career fueled his NASCAR habit. This is a Hall of Famer with three Super Bowl rings talking – the same guy who fielded drivers who went on to claim four different championships in NASCAR. NASCAR became his passion. He simply grew up, like so many Americans, in a culture that encouraged a love for cars, watching a sport that created an obsession with speed, risk, and challenge. He's a man who is very deep in his faith, a deeply patriotic American who is deeply in love with NASCAR.

There are entire families who catch the NASCAR bug. Take, for example, the Gilletts. They're very involved in everything from hockey to stock-car racing. They know racing is a costly sport and difficult to sponsor, but they also know that being involved in this type of sport puts them on the map in the eyes of the American people. These are driven men, in business and in sports. They go from one thing to the next. They climb one mountain, stand on the summit, and look for a higher mountain. NASCAR is one very tough mountain to climb, but if you want to be the very best, it's one from which you can't walk away.

These are not the days of Richard Petty when the competition was lower and one star could dominate the track. The competition is fierce and the cars are expertly made. That's what makes drivers like Jimmie Johnson and teams like Hendrick Motorsports so impressive. Being able to dominate for five years in the face of such strong competition requires that they never lose their edge. Winning isn't easy in NASCAR. And winning the Daytona 500 – with the costs of car engineering and maintenance, the logistics of sponsorship, the challenges and risks posed to drivers, and the length and difficulty of the championship – could be said to be more difficult than winning the Super Bowl or the World Series.

Taking the current economic climate into consideration, looking at the neutralized state of the NFL due to salary caps, and the financial pull of baseball teams like the Yankees, it's difficult to say how easy or hard it is to take a championship when there's so much going on. Yet if one could somehow have the same amount of money to work with and the best talent, winning a NASCAR race would certainly be more difficult. Granted, in the World Series you have to win four out of seven, which can be a great challenge for a team. A lot can happen in that time. Yet in motorsport racing, there is so much less control over what's going to happen – out on the track or inside the car. Drivers and teams don't have a great deal of control over the track, the car, or the competitors' vehicles. There's no telling what can happen – a blown tire, a wonky malfunction, or a sudden turn in the wrong direction by the car next to you can mean the difference between first place and twenty-first.

In NASCAR, you could win races most of the year and find yourself dominating the sport – then in those last ten races end up in an unexpected wreck that may not even be your fault. Your chance at the championship can vanish in a matter of minutes. It's the unpredictable nature of driving and of relying on a machine that makes NASCAR so difficult as a sport. Yet the car is the essence of NASCAR – you can't say NASCAR without car, just as you can't picture the United States without them.

Many Americans grow up around cars. I know I did. My father worked on cars as did his father. There are generations of proud Chevrolet and Ford owners in the United States, and they're often the same people who follow NASCAR and will do whatever they can to support American growth. That's what's so admirable about them. Of course, this strong devotion to U.S. business can occasionally lead to misunderstandings – like the fans' resistance to Toyota signing on as an official NASCAR sponsor. Many fans, who are natural supporters of American business and advocates for keeping jobs in the United States, didn't want that invasion. Even Jack Roush, the founder, CEO, and co-owner of Roush Fenway Racing, was resistant to opening the doors to an international car company before doing everything possible to make sure that we were supporting American business and economic growth. However, since Toyota actually works with Ford, we don't have to sacrifice anything by having them sponsor NASCAR. It doesn't mean that we're un-American and that we've lost our roots. NASCAR *is* America's roots, and keeping a hold on those roots is vital.

Personally, I think it was smart of NASCAR fans to show an initial resistance to this change. These are people who connect to American cars and corporations. Again, it all goes back to patriotism. The hands-on, hard-working Americans, from the farmers to the carpenters to the soldiers who make up a big part of the NASCAR community, are highly patriotic. And fans from all colors of collars like to connect to American cars and support American business. Fortunately, once everyone had a better understanding of the rules and the nature of the business venture, they realized that they weren't sacrificing anything. They were able to honor their roots while also branching out to sustain the future success of the sport.

I don't want to say that NASCAR fans are more patriotic than others, but I will say that they are more patriotic than most. Their sheer loyalty to the sport and to their country shows. The ratings we get are astounding. In one pre-race show – during a rained-out race, no less – we outdrew the ratings for basketball players Kobe Bryant and Lebron James. Even when the NASCAR ratings aren't doing well, other sports don't experience nearly that level of dedication.

At the beginning of the chapter I mentioned a very memorable, rained-out race – the Coca-Cola 600 on Memorial Day Weekend. That pre-race show, which I was broadcasting, outdrew the about 11.5 national baseball rating. We had a higher rating than America's favorite pastime. And that was just us broadcasters – the engines hadn't even started! How'd we do it? For one thing, we try to keep the broadcast homespun and down-to-earth, even though we are working through a bigger network. That's what the fans are looking for, and we have it. But we also got such high ratings during that Memorial Day weekend because we were interviewing fans' favorite drivers, talking about their favorite sport, and tying in patriotism with racing – something that our fans value quite a bit.

NASCAR fans will never apologize for being patriotic. So much of what NASCAR is is about being American, whether it's supporting American manufactured cars, enjoying quality time with the family on race weekends, or watching the spectacle of race day. What fan doesn't admire the modern, technological advancements that NASCAR showcases, evidence of the advancements that the United States has introduced to the world?

NASCAR is defined by America; it is truly America's sport. It's not corporate America's sport – all families can afford to be fans, no matter where they are or what they do for a living. And just like the rest of our country, NASCAR is growing and it's strong. Whether you're a savvy sports enthusiast like Joe Gibbs, a gearhead, a hard-working parent, or a kid who likes to watch cars burn rubber at high speeds, NASCAR has something for every American: a sense of pride. Watching America's finest cars and sharpest drivers out on the race track, supported and sponsored by our admirable companies, makes them proud to be American.

4

SPEED

Here in the U.S.A., we do things fast. We eat our fast food racing down highways while rushing to little league games from the office. There's no doubt about it: this is a fast-paced society. So it's no surprise that the United States is home to the sport of speed. There's a little speed demon in all of us.

If we're honest with ourselves, we'll admit that none of us goes the speed limit all the time, not in our nine-to-five lives and certainly not on the road. We love going over the limit. It's about pushing it to the edge. It's the roller coaster we all want to ride but we're a little bit afraid. NASCAR gives us that same rush.

Speed is something fans can connect to in NASCAR. It's the thrill felt when the pedal is pushed down, that feeling of control – two hands firmly gripping a smooth steering wheel, the rush of adrenaline and excitement. It's a feeling Americans can't have every day. In our daily lives, our inner speed demon is hampered by traffic jams, speed limits, flat tires, and mundane errands. So people go to the races – the one place where speed is not only condoned; it's praised.

In many ways, speed is very much a part of the American lifestyle. We are always moving, always going. We're lucky to grab a fast lunch or have time to whip together dinner in the evening (something that often ends up being quickly heated in the microwave). Yet, it's not just about living fast – it's about competition. We have to stay on top. We have to have the best schools, the fastest technology, the quickest turnaround, the most productive task force. We are a society that thrives on capitalism, and capitalism thrives on competition. We have to do it better and faster than everybody else and each other.

In racing, that ideology is physically embodied in two cars racing head to head down the track to prove, definitively, who is better and who is faster. Sure, there's a macho side of it, but it has everything to do with the fast-paced, capitalistic, competitive American culture that this sport comes from. Whatever the limit is, we have to go a little bit beyond, if for no other reason than to stay on top.

People often try to describe to me what it is they see and feel when they attend the races in person. They talk about the particular sound of the cars whipping past them. The bright colors of the cars blur, as in a photograph when you try to take a picture of something moving and the camera just can't catch it. But NASCAR, however fast it may be, leaves a lasting impression. It leaves a sensation that you just don't get anywhere else.

Actually, maybe it *does* compare to something else. Remember that first go-cart ride, or the first time you drove in a car with your buddies? Or that roller coaster or motorcycle ride when you finally got comfortable and said, "I want to take this a little bit faster"? It's human nature: we reach a limit and we want to go a little bit beyond it. We're all sixteen or seventeen, racing on a dirt road with our friends, yelling, "Go faster!" That love of speed, that competitive spirit and fast-paced culture is all-American, and it's what NASCAR is all about. We love going over the limit.

The question then becomes: How far above the limit can we go and stay inside the lines? How long before we get caught? How far can we go and how much can we get away with? We have our little ones in the backseat, our speed limits and responsibilities that keep our speedometers relatively low. NASCAR, though much less hampered by things of that nature, still has to abide by certain regulations.

Obviously the cars of today are a lot faster than the race cars of yesteryear, but they could be even faster. Restrictor plates, necessary for safety reasons, restrict the horsepower of NASCAR race cars at Daytona and Talladega. A restrictor plate is a thin metal plate with four holes that is placed between the carburetor and the engine to restrict airflow from the carburetor into the engine limiting the amount of power the engine is able to generate, which ultimately reduces the vehicle's speed.

In years past, race cars were similar to showroom cars and were thus less aerodynamic. (For 2013, the big four car manufacturers are introducing cars to the buying public that are very similar in style and looks to their counterparts on the race tracks and which will be distinguishable from the other manufacturers' race cars.) At that time it was safer to push the limit. Now cars have to be more closely monitored, which includes having the race car's horsepower kept in check. As much as we love speed, we have to be realistic about safety and how far we can push the boundaries. Operating within certain limitations means that we have to make certain sacrifices. For that reason, most speed records are usually set when a driver is qualifying. If drivers don't have to worry about other cars on the road, they have the freedom and the space to zoom around as fast as they like. They don't have to worry about wrecks or anyone getting in their way. Safety becomes less of a hindrance. As far as speed and safety are concerned, NASCAR has set up a fair ratio between the two, maxing out the speed while keeping the races as safe as possible. Yet still there are those who are tapped on the shoulder by their inner speed demons and can't resist the urge to go beyond the limit. There's always that temptation to out-do the competition, to go just a little faster.

In theory, a car could easily be built to go well in excess of 200 miles per hour, assuming that the car makes few turns and is traveling in an unobstructed path the majority of the time. There's nothing, save for restrictor plates and a set of stringent regulations, stopping teams from doing so. Like all sports and areas of competitiveness in our day and age, there are those who try to get ahead by cheating. Compared with the scandals that have affected some other sports, NASCAR has done a good job dealing with this issue. Since there is no union in NASCAR, officials have more control over the rules of the game and the punishments for violations. If they want to crack down, they crack down. They put the rules out there, and they enforce them the very best they can.

We care about the sport and we don't want to deal with a soured reputation.

In this day and age of steroids, drivers are also being scrutinized for cheating by way of drug use. This baffles many NASCAR fans and outsiders alike. What could a driver possibly take to enhance their performance other than a cup of coffee? There is a list of banned drugs in NASCAR, including particular stimulants. Stimulants are essentially like coffee except much, much stronger. Of course, NASCAR also enforces a stringent anti-drug policy that strictly forbids the misuse or abuse of any drug. This was violated by Jeremy Mayfield when he tested positive for methamphetamine, which probably didn't increase his ability to drive but did put him and other drivers on the track at risk. This was a very clear violation, but for a while people tried to give Mayfield the benefit of the doubt. Due to the many rules and regulations in NASCAR, sometimes while trying to navigate through confusing red tape or figuring out how to make a repair on a car in less than fourteen seconds, a certain amount of caution gets thrown to the wind. There just isn't time to leaf through a manual when you're going 180 miles per hour or jumping over the wall to fine-tune an engine. Just as with the National Collegiate Athletic Association (NCAA) and their recruiting rules, things come up. There are always new rules and restrictions that the team might not have thought of, since NASCAR regulates everything from the height of the roof and the length of the bumper to the specifics of the engine.

Through the course of a race, many pit stops are made. The parts of the car, which were carefully placed according to guidelines before the race, crumble, wear down or break. Teams have to come up with quick solutions under pressure. However, using illegal fuel or car parts, with full knowledge of its illegality, is cheating. That is treated with seriousness in NASCAR, and there's no excuse for it.

The body shop is where some of that monkey business goes on. If that's the case, the driver is less involved and the fault could be placed mostly on the team or the crew chief. At times, NASCAR teams are like a board room of well-paid attorneys – they look for loopholes and see if they can squeeze through them. In some instances, the driver may not be aware what the team is doing. As the saying goes, he just wants the hamburger; he doesn't care how you slaughter the cow. It can be hard to tell whether drivers are involved and how much to penalize them. It is plausible for a driver to deny responsibility for rule violations, especially if something was done in the body shop without his knowledge.

Still, many drivers are aware of what's going on with their vehicles, and ultimately their name is attached to that car and their team. It is *their* reputation at stake. They have to ask themselves if those extra miles per hour are really worth it, and if they should sacrifice speed for safety. If a driver is branded as a cheater, no matter how fast he's moving, that reputation will follow him for the rest of his career. It can take a lifetime to build a name for yourself in this sport, and just a matter of hours to lose it. Most teams look for that competitive edge, but they're not going to cheat to get it. Drivers have too much to risk.

In the early days of NASCAR, the driver was so involved and hands-on that he was part of the team fixing the car. Sometimes he knew the car better than they did. If there was cheating going on, he knew about that, too. However, back then, chances were that he didn't care. NASCAR was a sport of rebels. The saying used to be: "If you ain't cheatin', you ain't tryin'." It was an accepted part of the game.

Yet as the sport grew in popularity and the technology advanced, questions of safety began to be asked, and NASCAR started moving away from that mentality. The culture of cheating was very loud and clear, and I have to give credit to NASCAR for cracking down on it. They want teams to be innovative and competitive, but they don't want to hear that old saying anymore.

Nowadays teams are checking the manual and even studying it because NASCAR has been stricter.

They know how to bring the hammer down. Their attitude is: if you're going to play the game, it's up to you to know the rules.

In the case of flat-out cheating, the athlete has to ask themselves why they're playing the sport and if it's worth risking their reputation. The punishments for cheating used to be a lot more lenient; now that's not the case. As much as there is an incentive to be the fastest one on the track and win at all costs, a team can get penalized very quickly – not only by NASCAR officials, but also by their sponsors and, most importantly, by their fans. It may seem like fans have less power than NASCAR officials, but when you think about who gives this sport its ratings, who buys the memorabilia, and who is essentially writing everyone's paychecks, it's the fans. If they collectively dislike a driver, that driver's career will suffer considerably and could end altogether. Drivers have to choose between getting that extra speed and possibly tarnishing their reputation. They have to figure out how much that quick fix is worth.

That quick fix, however, can be mighty tempting. Let's say I walked up to you with a pill – something I had cooked up in my basement. Sure it's illegal and contains all kinds of damaging substances . . . but what if I told you it could solve all your problems and get you ahead in life? Americans are always looking for a quick fix, a way to beat out the competition fast.

Nowhere else in the world are get-rich-quick Ponzi schemes, lose-all-that-weight-in-a-week diets, and miracle pills so popular, which is why our infomercial market is so successful: it's crammed with fast fixes. We want to throw dinner in the microwave and have it come out as a five-course meal.

Our athletes aren't any different. If someone could give them a pill that promised better performance instantly but shaved countless years off their lives, they very well might overlook the finer details concerning their health and well-being in order to succeed (even if it was cheating). There's an old saying that is still whispered in modern locker rooms: it's fine if you cheat, but not if you get caught. It's all about whether or not you're willing to take that risk. And that's probably one risk drivers *shouldn't* be taking.

Sometimes, though, NASCAR drivers would be willing to accept greater risk for greater speed – and they're not alone in this. Everyone in the sport, from the sponsors to the fans, all want to push things to the max – to go a little faster to really taste danger. Drivers have already taken that pill. The drivers live fast. They agree to whatever rules are set, but some of them aren't as concerned about their safety as the authorities making the rules. They just want to race. Every weekend they put their lives on the line.

The athlete on the outside of the car who doesn't understand racing may snicker and say, "Well, you don't have to be in great shape and train the way I do – you're just sitting in a car." They don't realize the pressure that speed places on NASCAR drivers. They may be sitting in a car, but they're moving over 150 miles per hour with forty-two other cars crammed on the track with them. Combine that with car wrecks, and it becomes a true test of ability. Even if you're very good at what you do – even if you're the best – you're very vulnerable on the circuit. If someone on the track isn't good at what they do, you may have to pay for it by avoiding a bad driver, dropping back in the race, or avoiding collisions. It's a different kind of sport.

Many people don't realize or understand what it is that these drivers do. NASCAR isn't just fast driving. In fact, speed is just one aspect (albeit an important one) of racing, just one element that draws people in. Even though it's important and it's exciting, a true fan isn't merely attracted to cars circling race tracks really fast. If that were the case, NASCAR wouldn't have too many fans. If a driver is going to be successful, they need more than just speed. Fans can watch the races just for the speed and the crashes, but they'll be missing out on a lot if they don't come to appreciate the sport for its other aspects.

Certainly the first-time viewer may have trouble picking up on the finer points of racing. For example, in a race at Dover, Jimmie Johnson was racing head to head with Tony Stewart. This isn't anything out of the norm, but it's exciting to watch if you know who is driving. To a first-time viewer, it just looks like two cars racing. But if you know you're watching the top drivers, it's exciting. Johnson and Stewart are two of the best drivers in terms of the fundamentals of what they do under pressure, how they handle the lead, and how they handle a bad car that's dropping or a good car that's in front. It's more than how fast they can go, even if they know how to pick up speed. Johnson and Stewart aren't alone in their abilities; certainly Jeff Gordon joins their ranks, along with many other drivers, including great drivers of the past. Being a winning team is about more than how fast the car can go.

People often wonder how much skill is involved and who deserves credit for winning the race: the driver or the car he's racing. I've never been a driver and I've never been a crew chief, but after years of NASCAR broadcasting experience, and after getting to know racing intimately, I can say that if a driver wants to take the finish line, he has to have the skill to do it. That skill is tested when things go wrong. It's just like any other job. Whether you're a pilot, construction worker, doctor, mason, engineer, or working at a fast-paced office – no matter the business environment – the person who is most skilled is the one you want to work with and the one who can handle an emergency. When everything goes wrong, to whom can you turn? Who handles problems the best and who knows how to respond?

That's knowledge and that's skill. That's what separates the best drivers from good drivers and the men from the boys. If a coach is able to handle injuries on his team with efficiency and make the necessary adjustments to get through the game, that's good coaching. If a pitcher is having an off day, but manages to pull through, that's a talented pitcher. If there's a wreck or a mechanical crisis on the race track, the talented driver is the one who has the know-how and skill to handle his vehicle with grace.

In a major crash, it can be difficult to tell if anyone handled their vehicle with grace. It's hard to say who was reckless, who was being a speed demon, and who just got caught up in a bad situation. I'll see a wreck and at that moment I'll think I know whose fault it was, but when I go back and watch the replay enough times, I'll realize that the car was set up to crash. It may be an adjacent driver's fault or someone near the driver who swerved the wrong way or made a wrong move, which led to resulting mishaps on the part of other drivers. Sometimes drivers will even apologize to each other for mistakes like that. They know that they could have handled themselves better.

For the most part, the drivers in this sport know how to handle themselves. A good driver with a decent car and well-timed pit stops will make their way through the race with mild success. If the driver's car isn't the best or has problems or needs adjustments, that, when his true skill shines. If someone causes a wreck and he has to navigate his way through it, his abilities see him through.

The United States is no different. As we face difficult times, our leadership is tested; our country and all its actions are scrutinized. Anyone can be a great leader when the resources are available and foreign relations are on the up and up. But when the going gets tough, that's when we're tested. That's when we have to shine. It's not about speed and how fast the problems can get solved, although that is important. It's about how we handle ourselves under pressure. It's about really addressing and resolving issues. That's the test of a good driver and leader. At one point or another, we all have to face that kind of test.

People in other sports may just see a guy sitting in a car pressing a pedal, but here in NASCAR we know that the truly skilled driver is constantly testing himself and is constantly succeeding – and succeeding at a lightning-fast speed. For the first-time viewer, that may not be quite as clear, but the speed and the action are. The spectacle of speed, from the first time a fan sees a race on television to when they finally buy those tickets and see the cars flash by with their own two eyes, is a spectacle that never tires.

The sense of shock a first-timer has when confronted with the speed of the cars whizzing by and the noise of the engines roaring past can inspire both awe and fear. Some fans wonder, how fast can these cars go? The idea of one mistake, at those speeds, is more than scary. Some people get a little shaken at their first race, especially if they're up close. Others fantasize about being in the car and think about how they would drive, the turns they would make, and the feeling they would have behind the wheel. Once everyone adjusts to the race, they love the fear factor and the speed. People get comfortable with the idea of speed and will do whatever they can to get close to it, short of sitting behind the wheel themselves. The initial experience of going to a race can be life-changing. It certainly was for me.

Before I even reached the tracks I could see how massive the scene was going to be. Whether it's Martinsville, Virginia, or Talladega, Alabama, the track takes over the city. Cars fill the streets. I didn't realize before I went to races how big of a spectacle it truly is. Of course, I'd heard the numbers, but it didn't hit me how large the crowds really were until I stood in a crowd much larger than any for the Super Bowl – and that was at a regular race. People need golf carts just to get around the track because it's so massive. It's a microcosm, a city in and of itself.

When I was outside of the track, I felt like I might be at a circus or carnival. There were souvenir trucks and vendors selling food of all sorts. I could smell the rich, savory aroma of good American barbeque roasting in the campgrounds. Some fans had passes to go see the cars in the garage. That surprised me. In few other sports could fans see players before the game or get that close to the action. To me it was like opening the door to the New England Patriots' locker room before the big game.

Fans get to see and experience so much at the races. It's hard to get a bad seat. If you're up high you get to see the entire track, which you don't have a hope of seeing from down low because it's so gigantic. But from down low you can feel the cars rushing by and see the colors of the bright vehicles blur. Everyone picks their favorite driver. Sometimes there's a driver who people are rooting against, maybe a driver who's edging in on their driver's lead. Every time Dale Earnhardt Jr. circles the track there will be a few cheers.

The beginning and the end of the race are the biggest spectacles. At the beginning there's the anthem and the show that NASCAR makes of that, and then there's the final finish, that race for Victory Lane. In between the end and beginning, fans eat, cheer, and holler. Some grow listless and distracted; others are wide-eyed and attentive for the whole race. They know that in every race there's that one wreck or move that everyone talks about the next day, and they don't want to miss out on it. There is no rewind button. If they take their eyes off the track too long, they may miss that one spectacular moment, that crash, or that expert maneuver that gets the rest of the crowd on their feet and cheering.

It all seemed amazing to me at that first race. And then I went to the Daytona 500. There's no way to compare any other sporting event to it. The Daytona 500 is the cream of the crop in racing; I had never been to a race like it before. I had the idea that it was just going to be cars going around the track, but from the moment you pull into that parking space, you enter another world: the food, the vendors, the garage, the thousands and thousands of people, the sound of the cars, the excitement that pulsates through the air, and the drivers who seem to be superhuman. The smell of the oil and rubber on the track. The sound of cars screeching and scraping the walls. The blurring colors. You *see* speed.

I'll never lose that initial impression that I got from the Daytona 500, even if it was, at times, all a blur. Once you've been a part of something like that, you develop a need for it. A need for speed.

5

TEAMWORK

When we go to the movies, we admire the stars on the screen. When we turn on the news, we listen to what our president has accomplished. And when we watch sports, we look for our favorite quarterback or race car driver. Yet the true greatness of our country, whether we're in Hollywood, the White House, or a sports stadium, lies in the labor of the unsung heroes.

Behind every great film there are many layers of talent, from the writers who create the script to the directors who oversee the making of the film. Though we may only see that great Hollywood star on the screen at the end, in truth that actor is only one part of the process. The same is true in the White House. The president, being only one person, couldn't possibly be responsible for an entire country. He has countless aides and advisors working tediously to keep him informed and able to do his job.

On the NASCAR track, the driver is the star, the leader, and executer. And while he has to be very talented to get into that driver's seat, somebody had to make that seat and the car it's in. Someone has to repair it and coach him through mechanical malfunctions. Someone has to pay for those malfunctions and organize the pit crew and the team on which the driver relies. All these people work together as a team to make the sport of NASCAR possible. Without cooperation and teamwork, nothing would be possible in NASCAR, and nothing would be possible in America.

Teamwork is an all-American value. We're hardworking and we like to get the job done right. Everyone has their role to play, from Hollywood to Washington, from the farms of the Midwest to the boardrooms of New York City, to the races at Talladega. There are the people who design the buildings and those who work in them. There are the farmers who keep us fed and the teachers who educate our future generations. Sure, the president is important, but by no means is he more important than the rest of society. Everyone is making a contribution to our great nation, and teamwork is what keeps this country running like clockwork.

It's the same for NASCAR. Just like we're all a part of the team that makes up America, the driver is just one part of a complex network of people who work together to win a championship. The driver is the executer. He may be the final step in the process of winning the race, but he's not the only one leading that car to the finish line. That driver wouldn't be running to the finish line if he didn't have the financial support and engineering know-how to get his car on the track. In order to do that, he needs a good team behind him. One team can employ more than a hundred supporting staff. The cost of financing a team with the necessary talent and paying for the materials needed to build the car can be tremendous.

The economics of NASCAR revolve mainly around sponsorship. Sponsors play a major role in the sport, and finding a good one can make or break a team. You can't build a car and pay your staff if you don't have the money to do it. Then the team of mechanics has to be assembled long before the actual car is. These mechanics and engineers are among the most talented in the country. The team boss and crew chief will organize who is on the team and the pit crew. These decisions are pivotal to the outcome of the race and the well-being of the car, but are rarely given a second thought by NASCAR fans. And yet, having a good pit crew is crucial to the outcome of the race.

Well-trained and sharp-minded pit crew members are sought after and noted in the NASCAR industry. Just as major league teams trade prized players, pit-crew members can be lured onto other teams with higher pay. Their paychecks don't come close to the drivers' or that of a major league player, but they are highly valued. Every team knows that having the right crew members is the key to getting into Victory Lane. Races have been lost due to a loose lug nut or poorly fixed quarter-panel damage. Having a fast time is critical, and these pit crew members are put under an extraordinary amount of stress to make sure that it happens.

Sometimes it can be difficult to appreciate the work that the pit crew does when you're watching the driver blast down the track in full glory. However, I've always had an admiration for those who can work well under pressure, particularly with cars. Many people just don't have the natural skill to do that kind of work. I know I don't, though my brothers always have. There have been many times in my life when I've needed a pit crew of my own – like the time I nearly crashed on the interstate.

Early in my career, I was doing local television in New Orleans, filling in the five o'clock sports segments on the news. I was driving to work when I suddenly realized I had a flat tire. It certainly would have been nice to have a pit crew then, because I was no tire changer. Not wanting to be late for work, I pulled to the side of the road and quickly changed the front tire as I best could. As soon as I got back on the road and accelerated up to speed, the tire flew right off. A lesson that would be hammered home once I began broadcasting for NASCAR: success lies in the details.

Unfortunately, the drivers seem to get the most attention – not when the car is running well and the race is going smoothly, but when they make a mistake. That mistake, like a loose lug nut, is enough to throw a race. That lug nut and the guy who didn't tighten it are now infamous. The casual fan doesn't pay attention to the crew unless something goes wrong. That seems to be the sad case with someone who is not always front and center – the time the spotlight hits them is when they call attention to themselves with a major flop, such as a cashier who miscounts the money in the register or the construction worker who leaves the job half-finished or poorly done. Sometimes the gift of good labor isn't recognized until it's not there.

It's important to appreciate every team member, because each one is vital to the success of whole. The assembly line, which is what put the American car industry on the map and made faster manufacturing of cars possible, is a good example of the value of teamwork in American society and business. Everyone has a role to play, a car part to place in the vehicle. No one built the car alone – that would have been inefficient and taken far too long. Yet by working together and developing an effective system of doing so, our automotive industry was able to flourish and pump out vehicles quickly. Teamwork is essential to American business and industry, and it's essential to NASCAR. These pit crews work to the very best of their ability, and just like the hard-working Americans who keep our country running, they work behind the scenes and out of the limelight.

To be honest, there was a lot I didn't realize about pit crews until I got inside the NASCAR community and closer to them. The pit-crew members are really some of my favorite people to interact with in the sport. They're regular guys who probably shop at the same stores as everyone else and send their kids to the same schools. They live closer to the reality of everyday Americans. When their day starts, they don't sprint out of bed to run laps like pro athletes or fly stunt airplanes like some drivers. They start the day off shuffling to the kitchen to make a cup of coffee, just like everyone else. Then during the week they work at the shop, probably from nine to five like many other Americans, then head home for dinner. Yet somehow, on race day, they come together to form a super task force.

The crew is like a team of volunteer firefighters who spring into action on a moment's notice. They transform from your average next-door neighbors into a task force that is jumping over walls and working at high speeds in perilous conditions. They have to be on their toes, and they have to work together flawlessly in a short time. These crews are, in fact, perfectly choreographed. Joe Gibbs began videotaping pit crews and having them practice their moves, changing tires and refueling cars until their routine was fast and flawless. Every second is utilized, no movement wasted.

Even though everything is happening rather quickly, there are certain things fans can watch for when crews are doing their high-speed dance. Our broadcasting team tries its best to show what the pit crew is doing from every angle, giving fans bird's-eye views, close-ups, and low angles. We even time the crew and keep the clock up for fans to see.

There are many stages to the pit-stop process. First, the driver pulls into the pit stall, which is trickier than it sounds. They have to reduce their speed considerably otherwise they get penalized. Then the crew jumps into action. While one crew member is tearing off a windshield (instead of wasting time cleaning it, debris is removed quickly by installing windshield tear-offs onto the car that can be peeled off during pit stops), another is refueling the car, and another is tossing the driver water. While all this is happening, there could be major or minor repairs being made on the car; they may be hammering a fender or replacing worn parts. What fans can watch for, if they are observant and able to catch all this while it's happening, is the team's synchronization, how well and how quickly they work around each other. One of my favorite things to see them do is to change all four tires in seconds. Meanwhile, I'm notorious for not being able to change *one* tire efficiently.

I remember when I was seventeen and I first got my license. I was working a late radio shift in Miami, and I was driving home alone. My father had taught me it was important to help other motorists in peril and would always pull to the side of the road at the first sign of caution lights and a lifted hood. That night, there was a woman on the side of the road standing helplessly beside a wood-paneled station wagon. We tried working together to fix the tire, but we didn't quite have the expertise to get it done. I was just about to give up and offer to drive her home. In fact, I think I damaged the wood paneling on the side of her station wagon. Eventually, a trooper pulled to the side of the road and fixed the tire. My brothers always laugh at that story and say it's a good thing I'm a broadcaster.

When it comes to the pit crew changing a tire mid-race, it's an entirely different story. When it's all said and done, which is oftentimes in just a matter of seconds, the team members escape from either side of the car and get out of the way so the driver can take off. The driver has to maximize his speed in about fifteen seconds to get back into the race properly. Once he's back in the race after a good pit stop, the pit stop may have been quick enough to move the driver up several positions in the race.

For the difference that a good pit crew can make, they really should get more credit. They don't get the kind of attention they should. The credit usually goes to the driver or the crew chief, but the guys on the crew are just some of the many people who make up the team behind the driver and crew chief. These unheralded guys don't appear on any roster. They're working-class people who love being on a team. They wear helmets and safety gear then put themselves at risk doing what they do. They're living proof that nobody does it on their own.

In this country, we have learned to work together. That's how we've built our bridges and developed our great cities. We work hard together and we've learned to trust each other. We've learned to find jobs that we're good at and that we love, and then do them to the best of our ability. We all play our part. When you drive over a bridge or when you watch a race, you may not think about the people who made that bridge or assembled that car, but they make America possible. The pit crews make NASCAR possible at every single race.

As behind-the-scenes as these pit crews are, they have risen to glory on occasion. Something that everyone in NASCAR enjoys is All-Star week. For a lot of people in the NASCAR community, All-Star week is fun because it's less stressful and all the events during the weekend are non-points events (all other races give out points to the drivers that correlate to their finishing position, but during all-star week, only winning counts and no points are rewarded regardless of finishing position). The format of the NASCAR Sprint Pit Crew Challenge Presented by Craftsman is fairly straightforward. Teams that are participating in that year's NASCAR Sprint All-Star Race and past champion crews of the NASCAR Sprint Pit Crew Challenge get to compete in the event. If the twenty-four spots in the competition are not filled based on the previous qualifications, the remaining participants are selected in order of car-owner points standings until all the positions are filled. The top eight teams in the points standings (it doesn't matter whether a team was selected as a participant because they are a past champion or a participant in that year's all-star race) are given byes in the first round. Teams seeded ninth through twenty-fourth face off against each other, two at a time. Winners move on to the second round, where the crews seeded first through eighth also participate. The crews continue competing in one-on-one trials until there are only two teams left.

I think the NASCAR Sprint Pit Crew Challenge is a great addition to NASCAR. Finally fans get a chance to see what the over-the-wall crew members do during a race and get a closer look into the nuts and bolts of racing. The tasks are the same from round to round. Each crew will have a jackman raise and lower a car while a gas man fills a pre-determined amount of gas, which isn't really gas in this competition, into a different car and the tire changers and tire carriers complete the tasks they would normally complete during a routine pit stop. All these tasks are done simultaneously on different cars. After each crew member finishes the assigned task, he or she races to another race car located at one end of a small runway and starts pushing the race car toward the finish line. As more crew members finish their tasks they join their team already pushing the car toward the finish line. The first crew to push their car across the finish line moves on to the next round, or, in the case of the final round, wins the championship. I enjoy watching the pit crews battle it out because I do admire the work they do. As I can personally attest, not everyone has these are skills.

It's true I can't fix a car like they do in the pits, but I have my own part to play. Like my cameramen and the people on my broadcasting team who make our broadcasts possible, we're all a part of the NASCAR team. People make the cars, drivers race the cars (once someone fixes them), and we put it all on air so the fans can watch it and the sponsors can sell their products and pump money into the sport. Everyone works together, in their own way, to keep this sport alive. It's a very functional system, and every part of that system is important to keeping NASCAR strong.

Yet sometimes things don't go according to plan. Sometimes there's a teenager trying to change a flat and someone has to pull to the side of the road to help. That someone is the crew chief whose job is to be in control in times of catastrophe and keep the wheels of the race team turning.

When pit crews aren't in sync, the crew chief puts them back in order. The crew chief is on the radio with the driver, trying to help him figure out whether to make a pit stop and lose time to make necessary adjustments. He's a therapist and a cheerleader; he talks the driver through things, pushes him on. He really has to know the car and the driver in order to be able to work with him and coach him on.

In baseball and football, we know the names of the coaches. In football we even know the names of all the coordinators and assistant coaches. We recognize it's not just about the players and the star athletes anymore. Someone has to have the experience to know how to lay out the game plans in order for the team to win. Coaches operate, in many ways, in the same way that crew chiefs do.

A crew chief works with the driver to develop a winning strategy on the road: when to take stops, what to repair, and when to fix it. He decides whether or not to keep pushing on in the race; he's the angel hollering over the radio in the driver's ear. Crew chiefs have a lot to handle. You can have the best pit crew and an amazing driver, but if your crew chief can't keep things together, has a bad relationship with the driver, or can't diagnose the problems with the car himself – there's no way your team is going to Victory Lane.

There are some crew chiefs who have really made a name for themselves in the sport, such as Johnson's crew chief Chad Knaus. He guided Johnson to five consecutive NASCAR Sprint Cup championships. Knaus is clearly hard-working and his attention to detail, if you listen to his radio conversations with his driver, is impeccable. He's ready to make adjustments for the situation at hand. He understands when something goes wrong, knows his team, and realizes their strengths and weaknesses. He gets the car running right for the track that day, and he keeps it that way. He knows when to gamble with the fuel strategy, when to call the driver in for a pit stop, and when to wait for a caution flag. There's a good deal of strategizing that goes on in the pits, and teams need a sharp mind like Knaus's to lead them through the race. A good crew chief is irreplaceable.

Good teams know that every member is important, whether it's the driver, the crew chief, a pit-crew member, or supporting staff. They appreciate that getting good sponsors is important, and that they need their fans' support. Teamwork isn't possible without a good team. That's why Hendrick Motorsports is willing to spend good money on its teams and its cars, which makes it such a remarkable team in NASCAR. No surprise, then, that both Johnson and Knaus are a part of Hendrick Motorsports. Ever since Rick Hendrick started it in 1984, it has been a winning team. Gordon's No. 24 has crossed many a winning finish line as part of the Hendrick Motorsports team.

Good teams work well under pressure and persevere through tragedy. In October 2004, Hendrick Motorsports suffered a great loss when a plane crash claimed the lives of eight of their senior members and Hendrick's twin nieces. Imagine a team where some of the key players, the ones who hold the team together and organize the team, vanish in the blink of an eye. Only the strongest team would have the strength to pull together and keep going. When Johnson took the win later that day at the Subway 500 it was clear that the Hendrick Motorsports foundation was solid. The team was able to pull together in a time of sorrow and win.

Another great NASCAR team is Roush Fenway Racing. Jack Roush was a driver who had driven dragsters in his day. He somewhat introduced Mark Martin into the greater NASCAR circuit, as Martin was a little-known driver at the time. Bobby Allison may have suggested Martin to Roush. It's safe to say that it was probably skill, but it certainly wasn't by being famous. Sometimes, if you want to find the very best people, you should ignore the spotlight, and look for someone who is good and honest and talented. They aren't always the most recognizable or have the wealth and sponsorship behind them, at lesat until their talent is noticed. Someone has to be seeking out that talent. The owners who form the teams have to have an eye out for the best players, for the diamonds in the rough, the rookies and the veterans driving to the race track after years of hard work, sometimes without a lot of money to show for it. They can't always go for the people who are set in the game – those people already have teams and sponsors. They've already been discovered.

Martin turned out to be a great driver and a major key to the Hendrick's team's success. It's all about who you have on your team. Though Martin wasn't well-known when he started out, he certainly made a name for himself because he was given that chance. In the years since, Roush has added other drivers such as Matt Kenseth, Carl Edwards, and Greg Biffle to the team, and they've been winning ever since.

It should be noted that Martin has now joined forces with Michael Waltrip Racing, and although now on a different team, he will continue to be one of the top drivers, as he has been for many years.

A team needs all its players to succeed – crew chiefs, crew members, drivers, and owners. In the same respect, NASCAR depends on everyone, from its fans to its sponsors to the supportive families of the drivers and crew members. Just as a car needs all its parts to keep running, NASCAR needs every member of its community to function as a well-oiled machine. Teamwork is everything in NASCAR.

The emphasis on the value of a good team has always been a part of NASCAR, but in recent years that value has been magnified. Drivers are making a habit of thanking their crews when they win and giving credit where credit is due. They're always talking about what goes on back at the shop during the week before race day. They know that they are the stars on Sunday, but they remember who works seven days a week to make them shine.

Racing is a multi-person, collaborative process. Some drivers used to be more hands-on, but the sport has become much more complex and specialized. Now there has to be good communication between all these people, even if they're doing very different things. Crews ask for direct feedback from the driver, and the driver has to be a good communicator in order to give it. Good communication is essential for good teamwork. The driver can't just say that the car doesn't feel right; he has to work with the crew chief and figure out what's wrong and what they need to do about it. Sometimes the problem is obvious, but sometimes it isn't. In times like that, communication and good teamwork are everything. The driver and the team have to be able to work well together if they want to get that car up to speed. Everyone has to know how to work with others in this sport, even if they're driving solo.

From the fans to the sponsors, from the families who support their drivers and crews to the crew chiefs and the guys working in the pit box, everyone has a job to do. Everyone is fulfilling their role to be part of the finely tuned machine that is NASCAR. Of course, sponsors provide a large portion of the financial backing for the sport. Without our fans, there would be no reason to race; and without the driver and teams, there would be no one on the track. Sure, there may only be one driver in the driver's seat, but the driver didn't pay for the car himself, and he certainly can't change his car's tires quickly enough to get back in the race without losing too many positions. There are no one-man victories in NASCAR. It's the team that makes or breaks you on your way to Victory Lane.

6

M O N E Y

What if I told you that you could be a NASCAR driver? If I told you to get a team together and a car, and then pay a fee and prepare to compete, would you do it?

Many Americans can and have done just that. It's the American dream – just average guys one day, and NASCAR drivers the next. All drivers at all levels in NASCAR fill out a form and submit it with a résumé of past racing experience. Those who are approved and make it past this process race without sponsorship and are known as independent drivers. You could be out there – the pedal beneath your foot, Tony Stewart and Jimmie Johnson waiting at the starting line with you. Perhaps for just a second, the nose of your car could inch in front of theirs.

If this seems like a fairy tale, it's because it is. That doesn't mean that any of it isn't true. You can, with enough dedication and know-how, find yourself in a NASCAR race as an independent driver without sponsorship. Of course, you need the money to do it.

Some dreams are expensive to fulfill. The idea that you can simply work hard and achieve anything in this country doesn't quite embody the economic element of the struggle for success. After you add up the costs – getting the car ready, getting the team together, and paying the fees for the race – you quickly realize that some dreams come with a hefty price tag. If you want to get your wheels rolling, you'll need the expensive equipment and the necessary team.

Let's say you manage to do all of that. After developing the skill to drive 180 miles per hour safely, spending hundreds of thousands of dollars on getting a team and car together, and winning a handful of races ahead of time, you've sweated your way to a NASCAR race. It hasn't been cheap and it hasn't been easy, but you've made it without a sponsor.

The race starts. You blast off . . . well, not really. Your car isn't nearly as well built as Johnson's, Stewart's, or any other sponsored pro drivers' vehicles. You try your best just to stay with the pack for the first few laps, but eventually you fall behind. You get off the track. The race hasn't ended; in fact, it has barely begun. However, you're not upset – you're not even surprised.

Independent drivers who don't have the resources to put together a good crew, to pay the salaries of their workers, or to assemble a racing vehicle enter the race knowing that the odds are stacked against them. Yet some of them find a way to break through, which is another important aspect of NASCAR's appeal.

NASCAR drivers are driven by more than money. Take Tony Stewart for instance. When he's not on the race track pushing for the lead while being sponsored by wealthy corporations, he's at home racing with someone in his neighborhood. Other drivers spend their money on stunt airplanes or speedboats. They're always racing or getting into other high-speed, exciting sports.

These guys don't throw their money around – that type of behavior isn't something that's valued in the NASCAR community. You won't find these drivers rich one moment and then broke the next after they've recklessly spent everything they've earned. They take care of their families and their friends. Then they feed their passion by getting into extreme sports, fueling their love for speed and competition. Even if they have guaranteed contracts, a lot of these drivers would race for free (well, if someone *could* race for free). The money they earn goes right back into the sport. Sportsmanship and healthy competition seem to fade elsewhere in the sports world, but not in NASCAR. For these drivers, it really is about the sport, not the money.

That's something that is really admirable about NASCAR drivers, and it's part of what makes them role models for all of America. It's important that we remember where we come from and what it is we love. In a society moving a million miles a minute, it can be hard to remember what really matters. Sometimes it's even easy to forget why we're working for that paycheck. So many Americans work long and tedious hours to make ends meet, and at the end of the day, they don't have time to spend with their families. For many, the family dinner is becoming a thing of the past. Between homework, little league practice, dance lessons, overtime, and late nights at the office, the American family is excelling at nearly everything except finding that quality time to spend together.

Family and community have always gone hand in hand in NASCAR. The sport originated within a tight-knit community of people with strong values, and the family who started it all still holds to those values. That's one of the reasons they're still the reigning family of NASCAR.

The Frances, a model American family, keep NASCAR together. Bill France Sr., who started the company in 1948, passed the "keys" of the sport on to his son twenty years before he died in 1992. NASCAR, one of America's most watched, most loved, and most popular sports, is still run the same way it was when it first began over half a century ago. Not only that, but it is almost entirely family run. You've got Bill France Jr., who took over in 1972 and handed the presidency over to Mike Helton in 2000 (the first non-France to hold the position). In 2003, Bill Jr. handed over the responsibilities of CEO and chairman of the board to his son Brian.

Believe it or not, NASCAR is a family business, just like your neighborhood mom-and-pop store. These are the people who make the final decisions and lay out guidelines for the sport. Their strong values have really affected NASCAR. There is a sense of community, a clear set of core values, and a closeness to country and national pride. They have never forgotten about the fans, and I personally think that's what has made them so successful. Even as more and more money has come into NASCAR, the France family has remained true to its roots and true to the sport.

As so many small farms across America get bought out by large corporations and so many family businesses struggle to compete with big business, it's refreshing to find a family who has remained faithful to their business and succeeded in good times and bad. The France family has survived a fluctuating economy, withstood all the challenges of growing a business, and flourished. That's the American dream, and that's what the American family is all about.

The Frances aren't the only ones who have found that financial accomplishment is only achieved with hard work and dedication. Many of the owners and drivers in the sport are examples of that as well. They value hard work that is ethical and guided by American values. Like many other NASCAR owners, Roger Penske is someone who values the American tradition of hard work put into action to achieve the American dream. He may have already been financially successful in the trucking industry, but since he's been in NASCAR he has recruited drivers from a variety of different backgrounds.

Perhaps one of the greatest examples of American entrepreneurship in NASCAR is Richard Childress of Richard Childress Racing. He's currently one of the wealthiest men in North Carolina, the state that has become synonymous with NASCAR. He has his hands in several ventures, but years ago his hands were on the steering wheel of an old race car. His life path has been an interesting one. He started out as a driver – a replacement driver at that. He later started driving as an independent. Perhaps the race was different back then and you could go out there with enough courage and personal financial investment and make a name for yourself. Or maybe his climb to the top had more to do with hard work, dedication, and more than a little bit of luck.

At any rate, Childress was a top driver in the late 1970s. Eventually, he left racing as a driver, but never left the sport as a whole. Using his resources, he started his own racing team. Like many drivers of today, he didn't blow his money – he pumped it right back into the sport he loved. He is now a successful team owner and businessman, owning not only a race team, but engaging in several other profitable business ventures. Childress embodies American entrepreneurship. He's someone who is willing to innovate, take risks, and invest in the things that excite him.

If Childress can race independently and become a NASCAR tycoon, does that mean anyone can do it if they have the American spirit of entrepreneurship, and the patience and dedication to fill their piggy banks in preparation for racing day?

Maybe so, but more likely not. The economics of racing have changed since Childress was tearing around the tracks, and even more since racing first started. It began as a small sport, something that was open to people who simply loved cars and racing. It didn't always require as much money as it does today.

But as the sport has grown, so has the cost of participating. In 2009, according to NASCAR.com, teams were spending between $18 and $19 million, $5 million of which went to staff alone. And those aren't even the highest figures – winning teams usually spend more. Entry fees are about $4,000 per event in the NASCAR Sprint Cup Series, so for a season of racing the entry fees are over $140,000. Trucking is a bit cheaper; the NASCAR Camping World Truck Series is *only* about $27,000 per season.

Then there are license fees. When you get down to it, the economics of the sport do not make it an easy opportunity for passionate amateurs without substantial financial backing. It's one expensive American dream. So how does a normal, everyday American get behind the wheel and onto the race track? Well, even if you have the cash, you can't just back your race car onto pit road. NASCAR has a résumé committee headed up by former driver Brett Bodine; if you want to race, you've got to have your credentials in order and be approved to race.

After adding all the numbers together, it's easy to conclude that economically challenged people, whether they're from the city or the country, whether they're a minority or not, are going to have trouble getting into the sport. It's going to be a financial struggle for most anyone wanting to get into racing without the resources.

Darrell Waltrip is one NASCAR driver who would use go-karts and lawnmowers to get moving. He raced to win because he needed the money from the winning purse. Today, especially because so many drivers are starting out so young, someone needs to make that investment. It won't likely be a sponsor; it will be your parents or someone who has faith in you before you even have faith in yourself. NASCAR careers start on dirt paths in backyards and grow to local race tracks until, after jumping through many flaming hoops, winning countless races, and spending big dollars, an amateur is given a shot at racing on a major circuit. It takes a lot of support from family and friends to ever make it to that point.

Jeff Gordon, Tony Stewart, and their families are living proof that without that initial support, drivers don't stand a chance at getting onto the track – much less into Victory Lane. Jeff Gordon's dad built him a dirt track. Stewart's family went so far as to mortgage their house, just so that he could follow his dream. That is an unparalleled level of family devotion to a child's dream and future.

David Reutimann didn't start out young – though he had a long-standing professional interest in cars, his racing career started when he was an adult. Just five years before winning the Coca-Cola 600 at Charlotte Motor Speedway for the first time at the age of thirty-nine, Reutimann was working on cars. There's a

chance that even at a late age a driver can be successful and more than a one-hit wonder. However, winning
a championship is a bigger challenge. Still, if you want
to get out there and race with the big boys, it is possible if your bank account can take the hit. Getting
into driving race cars is a major investment of time,
energy, and money.

The path for a young person to rise to NASCAR
stardom isn't clear-cut. There are different levels of
competition, and the sport is not just for the kids.
You really can start at any age. Some people get their
children into go-kart racing and midget racing, which
is set up for various age groups. They can have their
children driving at the ages of five or six. By the time
they're eighteen, they have a sponsor and trophies to
show for their years of training. It's somewhat like
baseball with the little league, high school, and college teams, though some baseball players don't take
that route, just as many NASCAR drivers get into the
sport at later ages. No matter your age, one fact
remains the same: you need the financial support to
get going. You can't do it alone.

The drivers and owners aren't the only ones who
feel the financial pinch – fans and sponsors feel it,
too. NASCAR has always been a more affordable
option for sports fans, and they've been able to attract
people from all walks of life and all wallet sizes for
that very reason. However, the current state of the

economy has called for some cutbacks, and for many families and individuals, going out to see a race is a luxury. Even when money is tight, fans find a way to enjoy the sport, and that's what makes NASCAR so strong – even in lean times.

If we're going to discuss the hard times America is facing and the fiscal aspects of NASCAR, we have to look at the car industry and the sponsors who are the backbone of the sport. Car manufacturers and other sponsors have their hands full, negotiating the economic slowdown that began in 2008. As far as the NASCAR community has heard, they have a plan . . . even if no one actually knows what that plan is. Luckily, Toyota was there to pump some financial life into the sport. So while the days of Chevy, Ford, and Dodge aren't ending, they are not alone on the circuit.

From the time when our founding fathers came together with the hope of forming a nation around respectable principles and ideals, this country was created on dreams and forged by those who take the risks and have the courage to follow through on those dreams.

Competing in NASCAR is expensive, but the organization has taken certain steps in an attempt to make the sport less financially restrictive. The goal seems to be to make the sport less about how much money a team has and more about its talent. The executives at NASCAR have put together regulations, so that everything can be more cost effective for competitors. There is no union in NASCAR, and when they want to make changes to improve the race, they do it. With the newer cars, they've tried to make it more cost-effective. They've limited testing, which made developing a winning car very expensive. They're trying to make it so wealthier teams can't get too far ahead just based on their wallets

But the reality is teams that have more financial resources can get the best people. Just like any business, when you're trying to get ahead, having money helps a lot. These teams can afford the best parts and the best people to assemble, test, fix, and drive their vehicles, and they can invest more in testing and technical research. It's important to have a competitive balance in NASCAR, and in many ways, that balance is hard to achieve; however, NASCAR has cut back on how many cars a team can field each year. Beginning in 2010, they reduced the number of cars an owner can field to four, which was down from five in 2009. Before that, it was unlimited. If you want your car on track, you need money or sponsorship. Everyone wants sponsorship, but sponsors want winning cars to put their logos on for maximum exposure. Unfortunately, the only way you can get that winning car is if you have the money to assemble, fix, and race it, money that teams want to be getting from sponsors. It's a vicious cycle. Unless you have money to begin with, racing and winning is very challenging.

The sport doesn't coddle its drivers, and a lot of the people in the sport weren't fed their success with a silver spoon; they were certainly not pampered along the way. Nothing is handed to you in NASCAR. Just as every American has to work to achieve the American dream, these drivers have put everything on the line to get behind the wheel. A good number of them come from blue-collar backgrounds and don't have the same opportunities as other drivers with more money. When people talk about drivers who have been fed their success with a silver spoon, they are usually talking about how the driver just couldn't make it. Truth is, those drivers just don't have the grit to handle the sport. Drivers who succeed against all odds may make a lot of money, but they don't forget where they came from or who put them where they are today – their fans, their friends, and their family.

Drivers, rich or poor, hold on respectfully to their roots. They have been raised with certain morals that hold strong. Money doesn't change that. That kind of upbringing is what makes NASCAR drivers role models. There is not much negative news on NASCAR drivers because they are fundamentally straight arrows. The NASCAR community doesn't encourage that kind of behavior, whether it's the administration or the fans themselves. These drivers are taught, whether they're aware of it or not, a set of core American values that garners NASCAR some serious respect. Those values can be seen in every aspect of their lives, right down to how they spend their money.

Take, for instance, former driver Ward Burton, who invested his money in property to protect the environment. He's a native Virginian with a strong appreciation for the great American outdoors. Instead of buying a Hummer or a stretch limo, drivers invest their money in other ways. They're raised to appreciate hard-earned money and with a core set of American values that keep them spending their money not only wisely, but in meaningful ways.

Maybe so, but it's more about the overarching message. NASCAR likes to keep its races open to everyone – it likes the idea of an open sport. Even if you come out of nowheresville, it still believes you should have a chance to race. Americans love to relate to drivers and see everyday people on the track. It's the same idea as *American Idol*; we like to believe that our dreams can come true. NASCAR supports that.

As crazy as it may seem, some people do it to make money. Even stranger: they do it to make money and they succeed. It's not entirely clear how, but several very successful teams and drivers have started engaging in what has now become known as "start and park." They drive a few laps, earn a few points, and take home cash without having to worry about the costs of fixing the car to stay in the race. Their strategy and how exactly the money balances out are uncertain.

There's something admirable about it, really. It's the same creative spirit of American entrepreneurship that got NASCAR going in the first place. It's the same spirit that makes our country so innovative. The drive to succeed and make money has inspired great advancement both in our country and in the sport.

Money is said to be the root of all evil, but in a capitalist society, it has been at the heart of great advancement. NASCAR drivers and their attitude toward wealth really show that just because you make more money doesn't mean you have to change as a person. What's in your wallet doesn't have to change who you are inside. If you have the right morals and guiding principles, you can maintain your integrity – no matter how much money you have.

That's why NASCAR drivers are role models, not only for our future generations, but for our corporations and our nation as a whole today. These drivers have made great sacrifices; a lot of them don't come from wealthy backgrounds, but their dedication and their family's dedication has gotten them to the very top of a sport that is perhaps one of the most financially demanding in the world. All people, in the United States and in NASCAR alike, respect those

who have worked hard for what they have. The
American dream is a great one, and it can be achieved,
but no one is going to hand it to you. You have to
get behind the wheel and race after it. And at the end
of the day, it's worth the fight.

7

TECHNOLOGY

"Life looks pretty good from here, doesn't it?"

He was an all-American tough guy, like John Wayne wearing a racing helmet. Some people would say he had an aura. There was something about the way he walked and the way he wore his sunglasses. They called him "The Intimidator." The sun was setting behind him. The sky was painted in those same ol' magnificent colors. It's funny when I think about it – at the time I interviewed him, I didn't notice the fiery beauty of that sunset. It was only twenty-four hours later, when I sat stupid from shock, my mouth half-open, that I realized how meaningful Dale Earnhardt's words had been.

His life did look pretty good: he was the star of NASCAR, and he was loved. Some said he was the fastest man alive, somehow invincible. But on February 18, 2001, his invincibility ran out. Dale Earnhardt, NASCAR's seemingly invincible super-man, proved that human life is terrifyingly fragile.

His tragic end was met with disbelief and shock. Moments earlier, Earnhardt was full of life, speeding down the race track. Everyone was cheering with excitement, gripping the edges of their seats. It was the very end of the race. Darrell Waltrip was doing his first broadcast for FOX, while brother Michael was headed straight to the finish line. Darrell was naturally excited and bursting at the seams. Meanwhile, Earnhardt, who owned Michael's race car, was blocking other cars to help him win the race. Earnhardt wanted to be sure that his team would win. When Waltrip passed the finish line, followed by Dale Earnhardt Jr., the excitement had hit a climax. There had been a spectacular crash, a win, and a great competitive finish. It was a euphoric moment.

Yet that crash was no ordinary crash. The audience, still reeling from excitement, saw a victory turn into a tragic loss within seconds. A driver ran up to the car to check on Earnhardt. He turned away quickly.

We had all seen crashes before, often serious ones, and yet the driver would walk away unharmed. Drivers defy death. That is what we love about the sport. And if anyone could survive a crash, it was The Intimidator.

We tried to radio in as people approached the car. We watched; we zoomed in with our cameras. We waited to see a moving arm, a leg, a body jumping out of the car. There was nothing. Had there been a concussion? No one spoke. The medical professionals came out. For once our broadcast team didn't know what to say. We didn't know any more than the fans. The broadcast was ended and he was taken to a hospital.

Meanwhile, I was trying to prepare for the post-race show. How could I possibly prepare? What could I say? FOX went to the hospital and got the official word from NASCAR: Dale Earnhardt was dead. We waited for word from NASCAR and then had to come back on the air.

Nobody knew how to react. We were stunned. It was too painful to cry. Our mouths just hung open and no sound came out – a silent scream. We went from great excitement to *this*. More information was constantly coming in. I had just interviewed him that week. I had met several people who worked on his crew, and I thought of the people who grew up with him, his family. The cameras came on and I sat stiffly in front of them. Then our broadcasting crew delivered the sad report, on a day that was so exciting and joyful just a few hours earlier.

In response to Earnhardt's death, today NASCAR has built safety force fields around their drivers using technology. His death inspired a wave of technological advancements and new regulations in the sport to keep drivers safe and put NASCAR solidly in the twenty-first century. Everything from new safety restraint devices to new advancements in engine technology – even the way we broadcast – has changed. There have been many life-threatening crashes since Earnhardt's death from which drivers have been able to walk away. Even in death, he left an impact on the sport. Dale is still keeping the sport alive.

If that accident happened today instead of over a decade ago, it may have happened differently. People would have demanded more information and more information would have been available faster. There would have been cameras in the car and recorded radio transmissions between Earnhardt and the crew chief. "Was there something wrong with the car?" people would wonder, listening to the radio conversations. We live in an information age, and when there's a tragedy, we want that information. Even then, there were journalists who were at our doors to get access to more information. They wanted photos of the car and medical reports. At the time, that was all kept very private, maybe according to the family's wishes or for the sake of good taste.

New helmet regulations are just one example of NASCAR bringing its safety regulations up to speed. The advancements are numerous and growing. Now there's the HANS device that carefully cushions the driver's head and neck from impact. The windows in NASCAR cars have been changed to polycarbonate – a material originally used in fighter planes – to prevent shattering. All drivers wear fireproof uniforms, another important safety measure.

Even the way the seating is placed in the car has changed. Now, if a driver hits a wall from particular angles, he remains protected; the driver's seat has been moved toward the center of the car and further back to reduce impact on the driver if the car is hit from the front or the side. Since 1988 restrictor plates have been used at Daytona and Talladega. Plates are installed in the race car's engines to cut back on the amount of air traveling from the carburetor to the engine thus restricting the horsepower the engine can produce and decreasing the speed of the vehicles. Marshalls and safety teams exercise more caution; they're more alert and are watching for danger.

Safety has become a priority for NASCAR, and the technological advancements in the sport have made the act of driving safer. NASCAR has a lot to offer in technological advancement, not only for its fans and drivers, but for the country. Perhaps if these innovations were used off the race track, they could make for safer cars on our highways as well.

Advancement hasn't only come in the form of newer and more effective safety technology. In fact, the worry that many people have now is that there has been too *much* advancement in technology. The sport is becoming so advanced that NASCAR has to work to keep things from going on autopilot. We want drivers to have an influence and an impact. If there are too many high-tech tools and gadgets, it becomes more about the cars and technology a team can afford and less about the driver. There has to be that human element.

NASCAR also wants to keep the races fair. If it becomes too much about technology and who can afford it, then the races lose their human element. Sure, some teams can afford better cars – but NASCAR doesn't want it to be about who has more money. They're working hard to balance the sport competitively, allowing teams to compete and win based on more than the technology they have and the car they can afford to engineer. That's one of the reasons NASCAR uses the restrictor plate. By placing the device in NASCAR engines, they can keep the speeds at Daytona and Talladega down.

Speed isn't the only thing that NASCAR limits using technology. The engineers and mechanics working for these teams are some of the most creative and talented staff America's body shops have ever seen. They're constantly inventing new ways to make cars run faster, smoother, safer, and more efficiently. That's why NASCAR officials have to keep a close eye on all technological advancements in the sport to make sure that the competition is fair and balanced, and that the human element doesn't get lost. So NASCAR limits testing. They also regulate what type of fuel can be used in the cars. While this may seem trivial, fuel can make a big difference – especially when teams start using propylene oxide, which is a gel-like substance used in rocket fuel to help send their vehicles blasting to the finish line.

NASCAR is on top of all the latest technology – they have to be. Teams are working around the clock to get that competitive edge. They're constantly creating new ways to get to the finish line faster, like tinkering with aerodynamics: the way in which air flows around the car. Getting good aerodynamics is essential for a winning race car. By creating a vehicle that is smooth and streamline, engineers and mechanics are able to avoid the friction that occurs when air flow is disturbed – something as small as a candy wrapper can slow a car down by disturbing the air around it. When a car isn't streamline, air doesn't flow past it easily and it moves slower. These cars must be fine-tuned.

Nothing can get in the way of NASCAR's fastest automobiles, not even air. Sometimes, though, cars become too aerodynamic. In 1994, roof flaps had to be placed on cars to help prevent them from becoming airborne. Technology and expert engineering have made these cars go so fast that now we're just trying to keep them on the ground. In 2012, NASCAR went to fuel-injected engines, for a variety of reasons. First, they're more like the engines in the cars you and I drive, which is one of NASCAR's key attractions. (Okay, we don't have one seat and a roll bar in our cars, but you get the point.) Yes, it was easier for NASCAR crew members to work on vehicles with carburetors, and the traditionalists no doubt squawked when NASCAR mandated the change. But the new fuel-injected engines are more efficient, and efficiency is crucial in NASCAR.

In 2013, NASCAR car manufacturers are bringing their car models back to their roots. The new NASCAR vehicles that will be unveiled over the next year will look similar to the cars that fans can view and purchase off car dealership showroom floors. Each of the car makers that compete in NASCAR will now be distinguishable from each other, and this is one step closer to allowing auto manufacturer branding. This is something important for the re-engagement of fans and for continued fan loyalty – to see cars that resemble the ones they themselves could drive, have in their garages, or buy will create natural support for the fans of NASCAR.

The track design also affects the car's aerodynamics and how engineers approach the build of the vehicle. If a team is racing at Tennessee's popular Bristol Motor Speedway, they're going to have to prepare themselves for a short track and hard concrete. In Daytona or Talladega, the tracks are bigger and getting around them quickly is everything. In those situations, teams need good aerodynamics so they can move more quickly – every second counts. When teams prepare their cars, they design them with specific race tracks in mind.

Technology has taken the sport to the point where preparation, research, and good engineering are essential for a driver to be successful. It cuts time. Technology is used to get things done faster, just as it is in everyday America – we drink our coffee from the automatic espresso machine, make breakfast in two minutes in the microwave, multi-task by using an electric toothbrush while we dry our hair, and drive too fast to get to work on time. As a culture, we like to move fast, and technology saves valuable time.

That's why America is one of the most technologically advanced societies in the world. And that's why NASCAR is constantly advancing – we want to do things faster, and we're always trying to move ahead. We're racing into the future. The technology displayed in NASCAR is cutting-edge. That's what many fans love about NASCAR: the speed and the technology. They love learning about engineering innovations. That's what the gearhead is: a NASCAR fan with mechanical know-how and a passion for cars.

My brothers were the gearheads of the family. They knew cars and engines. They were mechanically minded and kept track of up-and-coming automotive technology. I wasn't a car guy in the same sense, and I'm still not. I know how to turn it off and turn it on. Yet, there are a lot of fans that live for this. For them, NASCAR offers a delectable smorgasbord of things to look at. These are people who take their lawnmowers and motorcycles and pull apart the engines – just for fun. They know the names of all the different parts, and they can tell you what they do and why they're important. They look at how things are fixed during the race and how teams make adjustments. They're like crew chiefs watching a race.

That's what separates NASCAR from all other sports. There's this technological element in it – it's where science and sportsmanship meet. It's America's most technologically advanced and scientific sport. Technology has a lot to do with the final result, and that's what fascinates gearheads.

Dale Earnhardt was one of the greatest race car drivers of all time. One of the hardest moments of my career came when we found out he'd passed as a result of wrecking in the 2001 Daytona 500.

The first family of NASCAR, the Frances (l–r) Amy France Helton, Sharon France, Jim France, Betty Jane France, Brian France, Amy France, and Lesa France Kennedy stand with statue of Bill France Jr. in front of Daytona International Speedway. Their strong family values have kept NASCAR humble over the years, while their keen business sense has helped it expand. (Photo by ISC Photography)

Mark Martin never ceases to amaze me. In his fifties now, he's still able to out-race drivers half his age.

Carl Edwards is a driver I greatly admire. His love of speed carries over into his off-track hobby of flying airplanes and helicopters.

The flyover that starts many NASCAR races is just one of the many ways the sport honors the men and women that keep our country safe.

NASCAR knows how much the military means to its drivers and fans, so they are often invited to take part in the pre-race ceremonies. This is the 75th division color guard from Fort Sill before the NASCAR Sprint Cup Series Samsung Mobile 500 at Texas Motor Speedway.

Jimmie Johnson and his crew chief, Chad Knaus, talk before the NASCAR Sprint Cup Series Amp Energy 500 at Talladega Super-speedway on October 5, 2008. Knaus is one of the best crew chiefs in the business, with him calling the shots, Johnson has won five consecutive championships.

Mark Martin's pit crew is one of the best in the business. These unsung heroes are essential to NASCAR, just as the folks behind the scenes in America are essential to help keep America running.

NASCAR fans are proud of their patriotism, and it's always shown in the pre-race ceremonies. The singing of the National Anthem is especially powerful. There's nothing quite like being with thousands of fans and patriots, singing our great nation's anthem to start the races.

Brad Keselowski is handed an American flag to pay tribute after winning the NASCAR Nationwide Series Kansas Lottery 300 at Kansas Speedway. I've always admired Brad's poise and ability on the track, as well as his love for our country.

Richard Childress is one of the owners I admire the most in the business. He started as a driver before he moved into team ownership. He has always done what he can to make NASCAR a better sport, reinvesting his earning in developing great teams. That loyalty is one of the things that make NASCAR, and America, great.

It took me a while to break into the close-knit NASCAR community, but they let me know once I was in. Here I am with Jeff Hammonds getting a shower courtesy of Dale Earnhardt Jr.'s crew after they won the NASCAR Sprint Cup Chevy American Revolution 400 on May 15, 2004.

However, the sport isn't just for the mechanically minded. Even people who just like speed and competition or fans who enjoy the human element of the race can appreciate the skill it takes for a driver to win. They can enjoy the ambience that the races offer, the spectacle, the sounds of engines purring, and the people around them. Every fan is a part of the sport. Our broadcasting team has made sure that all fans have an opportunity to learn what's going on and enjoy the races – even if they have no idea what's under the hood of their car.

Our broadcasting coverage of the sport has really helped NASCAR grow. Our approach keeps it simple: we ask the questions with everyone in mind. If our fans know about the engines and the cars, they won't find themselves bored or alienated, but at the same time we try to keep our fans well-informed. We use diagrams and real-life vehicles to explain what's going on and what technology is being used in the race. On top of that, we have a crew chief and driver on our team to give us the inside scoop.

Between Jeff Hammond, Larry McReynolds, and me, we make sure that NASCAR fans know what's going on. Our team will physically go in and show the engine, point out the parts, and explain what they are. We keep the less-knowledgeable fan on top of what's going on, yet manage to keep everyone entertained and engaged. Even people who know a lot often want more information, and this is where they get it. Fans want to learn. We've been working at this for twelve years, and by now we've become a part of the race.

To take one example: fans listening in on a crew chief and driver talking might hear the driver say the car is "pushing" or "loose." We have to translate. We'll explain that pushing is when the car is tight and isn't moving smoothly, and that loose is when the car slides too much and the driver feels he has less control over the vehicle. On the race track, the computers aren't there to diagnose the problem. The driver has to explain vehicle malfunctions to his crew chief. Sometimes the problem is difficult to communicate. It's like a doctor and a patient: the crew chief listens as the driver describes the symptoms. Then the crew chief prescribes a solution.

Meanwhile, the fans try to figure out what's up and why the driver is headed to pit road. We explain what's going on so that fans will understand. Then the fan knows why the team had to go in for a pit stop to adjust the car. Sometimes it can get complicated. We know a big portion of our fans aren't gearheads, so we try to make our explanations simple. That way fans don't have to be engineers or know about the latest technology to enjoy NASCAR. As a result, we've drawn a lot of fans to the sport.

We've gotten a good deal of positive feedback from fans about our broadcast's display of technology. We have loyal viewers, not only because they like what we're doing, but because they like us. Being a good broadcaster and attracting fans is all about having a personality that will draw them in. You're sitting in their living room and talking for hours on end – if they don't like you, you don't have a show. We have Darrell Waltrip, the former driver, who is NASCAR's Terry Bradshaw. We have Jeff Hammond and Larry McReynolds. In addition, our team employs a great staff of pit-crew reporters. We've been successful because our staff is deeply involved in the sport, well-informed, and also because we like to have fun with each other. We each know how to play our roles well. Fans are going to get their questions asked and answered in a fun way. They're going to enjoy watching, and that's what NASCAR is all about.

Whether they're into the details of it or not, fans love the technology. It's just plain fun. You go to a race and you hear the sounds of the engines roaring and you get that feeling. The audio transmissions come buzzing on, and we get fans listening in on the driver's conversations with the crew chief, as if they're in the cars with the driver themselves. They may overhear a driver asking for a banana or some chips at the next pit stop. It's funny to think of Stewart or Earnhardt Jr. munching on chips at 180 miles per hour, but sometimes that's the way it goes. Fans are right there on the track, in the car – even if they're at home. They love it. It puts them closer to their drivers.

Few sports translate as well to the screen. Some don't translate to TV successfully at all. Hockey is a sport I always prefer to see in person; the television broadcast just isn't the same for me. Football does a good job of being entertaining on the set, but baseball is somehow better in the stadium. With NASCAR, there isn't a place we can't put a camera. Whether you're reclining lazily in your easy chair or gripping the edge of your seat, you're on the track with the drivers. You're right there.

That's why our fans love the way we broadcast. We put the race track in your living room. One of the most popular parts of our broadcast is "Crank It Up": we broadcasters close our mouths and let the cars do the talking. It's the natural sound of the track. People at home with surround sound can crank up the volume and experience the races. They can really get the feel of the race. Using every camera angle pos- sible and our carefully placed microphones, we're able to put our fans everywhere on the track. They see every angle, watch the cars whiz by, and hear them roaring down the track.

NASCAR knows that many of its fans can't always make it out to the races, and they've been very coop- erative with FOX in that regard. We've seen a good deal of evolution in broadcasting coverage as a result.

NASCAR let FOX put cameras onto the tracks so viewers can see the cars rolling, crashing, and crossing the finish line from every perspective. There are cameras inside the cars, so the race can be seen and heard from the viewpoint of the driver. You hear the crash and the sound of the tires screeching. You hear the radio transmissions. That's the kind of broadcasting technology on which the fans depend. It's all about getting them as close to the action as possible.

That's what makes "Crank It Up" so popular. Fans feel like they're really at the race. Even as a broadcaster, I have to say it's nice to hear the cars. Our team knows that our fans want to be informed, but they also want to watch the race. We keep our fans informed – we weave in our conversations – but we make sure the fans don't miss out on the action. On the radio I'd have to describe everything, but with television's visual and audio clarity, my job as an announcer is simply to enhance things. People need to be able to hear the crew chief talking. Those are the moments that we don't want to talk over.

Sometimes, if we're paying attention, we'll catch a driver and crew chief arguing. The crew chief might say something like, "You should come in for some fresh tires," to which the driver will stubbornly reply, "No, I want to stay out here." The crew chief will yell back in frustration, "Well, I'm in charge – get your butt in here, or stay out there and it's your own neck. You're on the line," he'll say. I don't want to talk through that. If there's a moment after the exchange, I'll give an opinion to enhance the broadcast. But if an announcer talks too much, it can ruin the broadcast. With the broadcasting technology we have today, there's so much that doesn't need to be communicated by an announcer. The fan can hear and see a lot of what's going on independently. As technology advances, fans are able to get closer and closer to the races.

As the races have modernized, so have the broadcasts. If someone were to go back to the first televised version of the sport, they would see something entirely different. There's a certain charm about those old broadcasts. Yet, they just didn't have the ability to get their cameras in all the places we do, to get access to the radio conversations between the driver and the crew, and to put their fans as close to the action. Technology has taken NASCAR to the next level, and broadcasting coverage has had to keep up to make sure that fans don't miss a thing.

As broadcasting technology grows, so does the concern that cameras might catch more than they should. With the in-car cameras, some of the drivers worry about their privacy. An in-car camera is only a few pounds. It's a small discus – it resembles something you might see on a James Bond film. There's no way that these little devices are weighing the car down or are any distraction to the driver. Yet some drivers ask that the cameras not be in the car. They just don't want to be watched all the time, which is understandable. They're already being watched and filmed by thousands; do we really need one more camera? Imagine being watched while you work, being filmed from every angle. It could get a little nerve-racking. These days, that's the reality of live sports television. It's true reality television because it's unscripted and the viewers are right there. Most drivers are cooperative and consider the multitude of cameras just a part of the job.

Still, the concern for privacy isn't unfounded. There have been situations when things have been caught on camera that should never be aired. We had a situation with a driver who crashed and suffered a concussion. The camera caught it, but we never aired it. You have to be respectful of the drivers and the fans. With cameras everywhere, they sometimes catch things that should be kept private. It's a situation that calls for discretion, which is something that our broadcasting team definitely has.

FOX respects NASCAR drivers, their privacy, and their viewers. This is quality entertainment and a family sport; we don't want to show anything inappropriate. We may catch a car hitting a wall and catching fire, and we might see something we'd rather not see. It's our broadcasting team that then makes an adjustment. The first broadcast that I covered was the 2001 Daytona 500. One of Dale Earnhardt's teams was winning and he was running third when his car crashed. We showed the wreck. At that time we didn't know that it was any different than any other wreck. Another driver ran up to the car, and I saw him quickly run away. We had to carefully edit the shots. We want to make sure we're not showing anything gory or too extreme. Until we know what's going on, we have to wait before making an announcement.

At the time of Earnhardt's death, we didn't have the same technology as we do today, and there was less information available. We didn't have the in-car camera in operation. While it would have helped us understand his death better, the in-car camera footage would never have made the air. We edit what we catch on camera before we put it out for the whole world to see.

Yet with the rise in popular communication technology today, it's hard to stop information from leaking out. There are too many fans able to take photos, record video, and make phone calls for us to be able to stop the flow of information. When Carl Edwards had his spectacular crash in Talladega, people had phones and cameras. They got pictures of the crash the instant that it happened. One of the women who witnessed the crash was in the news within minutes. She was attending her first race.

What baffled me as a sports newsman, however, was the fact that the word was out on the Internet minutes after the race ended – without the winner even being announced. With the growth of technology and the fast rate at which we can communicate with each other, it's hard to keep anything quiet for long.

Technology is great. It makes our cars faster and our broadcasts better. It keeps us in touch with one another. It makes our races safer. But Dale Earnhardt's death was far from simple – it was a tragedy that changed the face of the sport. In the years since, NASCAR has turned its focus toward harnessing technology in a way that maximizes safety for the drivers while providing an unparalleled level of transparency for the fans. The result is, hopefully, a sport that is safe and technologically advanced while still being human. It can be difficult to retain the human element amid America's fast-paced, technology-driven society and NASCAR's mechanically minded culture. But as the sport continues to evolve, it is constantly finding new ways to strike that perfect balance between man and machine.

TRADITION

ack is your average American kid. On the weekends, when he's not at school, he's in front of the TV. But he isn't watching cartoons like many kids; he's learning about the ins and outs of engines and listening in on crew chiefs and drivers as they talk back and forth on the radio about the transmission in their cars.

Before the race starts, he lines up his own cars. Although they are no bigger than his little hands, they closely resemble the NASCAR lineup, which he tries his best to mirror. He has taken great care to collect the most colorful race cars. He does not choose his drivers based on name, but rather on the color and appearance of their vehicles. Just as the race is about to start, he says, "Gentlemen, start your engines!" Though he is only four, this little NASCAR fan has grown more and more knowledgeable about the sport.

It all started when his father and my friend, Shaun Farnham, happened to have a race on. After that first race, the rest was history – it's like the floodgates opened and there was no stopping him. Little Jack has now become perhaps more knowledgeable than his father, watching the race with dedication every week. Farnham, a sportscaster like myself, spends quality time with his son, bringing him to radio shows and making him a part of the sports world. That world is not only the way he and I make our livings, but a community that we are a part of and that we will pass on.

That's why NASCAR continues to grow despite economic uncertainties and new trends in the sports world. It's a family sport and a family tradition. It's a way to impart values, such as teamwork and dedication, to kids like Jack. NASCAR is passed down generation by generation. That's what keeps it strong.

NASCAR has stood the test of time. It's been around for over sixty years and isn't going anywhere anytime soon. It's mindboggling to think that a sport that started as a result of an illegal activity could turn into the all-American family tradition that NASCAR is today.

Car racing originated on the dirt roads of the American South. Those early drivers weren't the shining role models we have today. They were rebels and bootleggers transporting illegal moonshine to thirsty customers. They were the original speed demons. Picture two cars with two hell-raisers behind the wheels, eyeing each other, with jugs of homemade booze in the back of their vehicles as a couple of townsfolk watch with anticipation. How did that turn into NASCAR?

Well, those men and men like them continued to race. Eventually, their kids got involved, and so did their communities. Suddenly they realized that racing had potential as a sport and decided to dedicate space to it. Soon enough, there were tracks, and families were going to the races.

Those families and their descendants are still going to the races today. Generation after generation, they keep coming. It's become more than a hobby or a casual interest: it's an all-out tradition. That's why NASCAR, more than any other sport, has a very strong sense of community. It's a family.

I know that when I first got involved with the sport, I found the community a bit intimidating. It's always hard to make yourself a part of a community that you're not familiar with or connected to. These fans are the same people whose grandparents and great-grandparents were out on those dirt roads and sitting in the stands of some of the very first tracks ever constructed for the purpose of racing. It's no wonder that when I walked into a NASCAR race track for the first time, I felt like a fish out of water.

When first-timers don't have any connection to the NASCAR community, they quickly realize that NASCAR fans aren't your typical enthusiasts – it's a strongly dedicated community with values. At first this may be daunting, but as long as there's someone there willing to let that person in, and the first-timer dedicates time to understanding the sport and culture of NASCAR, he or she is able to become a part of it all.

More and more fans become a part of the NASCAR family every year. The sport manages to maintain its fan base. Even if your grandfather wasn't a moonshiner, biting the dust in the 1940s on the southern back roads, you can still be a part of this sports community. You can enjoy the culture and the atmosphere while becoming a part of a community that upholds the great American tradition of racing. If NASCAR were a closed community, it wouldn't be growing as a sport and attracting new fans from across the country. While the original image as a rebellious southern sport has faded, it hasn't lost its charm or grassroots core. Fans and families have remained true to the sport and make up much of the NASCAR community.

In the last five to ten years, NASCAR has worked to get tracks in more places in order to bring the sport to other parts of the country. While some of the older tracks still exist, there are other tracks within driving distance from tracks that may have lost races in the past. Recently, there has been some revival on the track in Rockingham, North Carolina. It was at one point just a test track for NASCAR race cars; since it was not on the NASCAR circuit, testing was unlimited. However, in 2011, it was announced that Rockingham was to install Steel and Foam Energy Reduction (SAFER) barrier along the track walls to improve driver safety. Now, the NASCAR Camping World Truck Series will be held there in 2012. NASCAR didn't pull its attention away with bad intentions. It wants to keep its grassroots core and stay true to the fans who keep the sport strong. At the same time, it welcomes newcomers and people that might be interested in the sport, but who don't come from that culture or have the same family history. It really is a sport that is both old and new at the same time. Though deeply rooted in tradition, NASCAR has become very modern.

These days, young people and teenagers have become a major part of the sport. They get into the races then bring their friends. It's not just because their parents like it. Not only has the sport recruited younger drivers and new technology, NASCAR is a real-life version of video games. Believe it or not, games have really helped both the fans and the young drivers. Gaming helps them understand the different tracks. The young fans get to the race track and know what to expect from playing the game, and the young drivers apply that knowledge and skill to their racing. They're in touch with technology and are able to use it, not only for virtual entertainment, but also in the real races.

That's why there are so many young fans out there who may not have the same familial connection that a lot of folks have, but who are knowledgeable and have an appreciation for the sport at an early age. There are twelve- and thirteen-year-olds who step on to the track for the first time in their lives yet know every twist and turn from what they've read, played, and watched on TV. This generation is really using technology as a tool to get knowledgeable faster. We have young drivers who have raced less but know more. Drivers are training younger and younger.

It's essential for young drivers to have family support for that very reason. They need to be raised in the culture and get exposed to the sport early on in order to train. It's hard to imagine that a teenager is expected to be racing professionally while their friends are just learning to drive. And yet, it happens. The racing world is being driven to new extremes.

NASCAR and drivers know that the younger generation makes up a considerable part of their fan base, and they reach out to them in ways that young people enjoy. Dale Earnhardt Jr. and Martin Truex Jr. race fans online. The fans know that they're racing against these actual drivers on a track that replicates Daytona or Bristol. The drivers love it, and the fans are ecstatic to be racing against these multi-championship-winning heroes. Sometimes they even win. Though they're not out on the real track, many of skills required to win on a virtual track are similar to those needed to win an actual race. You have to be able to strategize and guide the vehicle to that finish line, and that's the same whether it's real or just a game.

When fans race against their heroes, it connects them to the sport on a more intimate level. They're racing against their favorite driver, just like they play video games with their best friends. Virtual racing teaches the young people more about the sport, and it draws them into it in a way that was not available to their parents when they were growing up. This younger generation connects to the sport in their own way. They may not be racing down dirt paths like their forefathers, but they are contributing to the NASCAR community. Someday, their own children are sure to find their own way of connecting to the sport.

NASCAR is for everyone, young or old. Everyone has their own way of engaging with it. It's a multi-generational family. One week you have a forty-year-old driver, like Greg Biffle, mature and experienced, in Victory Lane, and the next week you have the twenty-two-year-old Joey Logano stealing the win. Although NASCAR has a minimum age requirement of eighteen, age is a less important factor when considering talent and skill. It's a sport that takes focus, endurance, and strategy; there's no age limit on that.

There's something very American about the idea that anybody can race at nearly any age. There are people in this country earning degrees in their sixties and seventies. We're taking better care of themselves, living and working longer, and "getting into the game" at later stages – no matter what that game may be. In response to that trend, NASCAR has managed to create a sport that can be entered at any age.

Another reason NASCAR links generations is because it is a family sport that fathers can share their sons. My friend Shaun shares with his son Jack. Mark Martin brings his boy to the races with him all the time. The Earnhardts have been in racing for generations. Even if they weren't star drivers at first, it's something that their family has gotten better and better at over time. For many families, an interest in cars and a passion for racing is something that is homegrown and passed down from generation to generation.

Just as there are generations of drivers, there are generations of families on crews as crew chiefs and engine builders. One family member gets involved, and suddenly everyone in that family is going to the races. NASCAR draws in entire communities. What the sport does for the economy of the greater Charlotte area is incredible – from bringing fans to the races to employing hundreds of locals. It creates a community. Although in the last ten to fifteen years NASCAR has welcomed more fans and thus more outside people into the working community, jobs often do stay in families, a true testament to the vibrant legacy of the sport.

There are plenty of examples of families who've handed down the honor of being a NASCAR driver. That may not mean that just because your father is a great driver that you will be a great driver, but a certain level of interest and innate ability may be there. Look at the Waltrip brothers. Darrell Waltrip is a multi-championship winning NASCAR driver. He won the Daytona 500, and he won NASCAR Sprint Cup Series championships – not once, not twice, but three times. He now broadcasts for NASCAR on FOX, and at one point he was announcing his brother's wins. His younger brother Michael Waltrip, also a well-known driver, now owns a racing team. The

Waltrip brothers are great examples of how racing is contagious in families. One person gets hooked and then the whole family gets involved.

Driving isn't the only NASCAR profession handed down through the generations. People who work on pit crews, drive the rigs for the teams, and work in the shop preparing the engine for the next week are often the children of people who have worked in the NASCAR industry. Jobs at all levels seem to be very family-oriented. One reason for this is because of the NASCAR working culture. Many of these professions are very demanding, requiring a strong interest in the sport and certain know-how. Those are qualities some outsiders might not possess.

Also, NASCAR teams travel from track to track. The nomadic lifestyle can be difficult for families, so team members bring them along. The family needs to be used to that kind of lifestyle and enjoy it; it's a learned preference. If they can't get used to it, then they won't be able to be a part of it and work on the NASCAR team. That means teams have to find a home not in a house or in a particular location, but in each other. If your family has already been a part of that community and team, then it's easier for you to adjust. The fact that many positions on teams get handed down in families makes logical sense.

NASCAR is a traveling road show, moving from track to track for each racing event. These families and crew members get close to one another and become like an extended family. They're around each other all the time, living and working together. They travel and live in motor homes. There's little more than a brief break for the holiday season, and then drivers are back on the track and their crews are back on the road. They really have to make a community and a family while they're out there. Most drivers spend just a few days at each track – they fly to the track right in time for practice and qualifying and then fly out immediately following the race. But while they are there, they find a new home for themselves on the race track and the open road, and their family is their crew and their race team.

There is a family-like closeness between crew members. Everyone that's out on the road together is part of that family, whether it's the drivers of the big trucks that carry all the race cars or the NASCAR drivers themselves. They pull into race tracks and they set up little communities, riding around in golf carts and preparing for the race until the race is over. This may seem like a strenuous lifestyle, but when you work and live with your friends and family, it becomes a community. Your home is everywhere you go. NASCAR is, in nearly every respect, a truly family-oriented sport.

I had the chance to spend some time with Bill France Jr. before he passed away, and I caught a glimpse of NASCAR's first family. The members of the France family have become role models of American royalty. NASCAR is their kingdom and, like any royal family, they want to make sure their people are content and well taken care of. They keep the fans, drivers, and their families constantly in mind. Guided by American values and morals, they answer to a higher authority. When it comes time to make a decision between right and wrong, they take other people's advice, but they're the ones to make the final decision.

The Frances make a lot of tough choices, and they always seem to make the right ones, basing their decisions on what is good for the sport. If they have to kick certain people out for breaking the rules, they do it. If they have to make certain decisions based on economics, they make the cuts they need to make. They cooperate with companies for the sake of sponsorship, but they make their own business decisions. It's a very effective way of getting things done.

The executive team, working under the Frances, has brought some truly great sponsors on board that have really helped the sport, like the Nationwide Insurance Company, which now sponsors what used to be known as the NASCAR Busch Series. The France family is powerful and successful, but they know who they are and where they've come from. They're not misguided or distracted by economic success.

The family uses its power only if it has to, and does so quietly, carefully, and judiciously. The Frances don't flash their money around, either. They've worked hard for what they earned and they're surely proud of it, but there's a certain culture that NASCAR fans, drivers, and owners respect; one that honors the working class and remains connected to the humble American grassroots. Money and power won't ever change that – no matter how big the sport gets. Having more money means they can help their families and the people they love live a bit better. The France family makes money, supports their family, and invests in the sport.

Only in America could a small car racing company, which was a fledgling family business, develop into a major power in sports. The NFL, NBA, and nearly every other major sport in the world have unions and corporate powers that call the shots, but NASCAR is just the France family. They work personally with the drivers, owners, sponsors, and teams. At the end of the day, they make the final calls. The sport rests on their shoulders.

That kind of pressure can really test a family. Before Bill France Jr. passed away in 2007, his son Brian had already been handed the reins of NASCAR as the CEO and chairman of the board. Mike Helton was named president in 2000, and to date, he is the first and only non-France family member in that role.

Today, everyone in the family has the opportunity to be involved as much as they want. For Brian and the France family, their main concern is to run things the way his dad would have wanted. The family may have its own disagreements, but as far as I have seen, they don't have issues with greed or power-hunger. Those are the things that easily tear families and businesses apart. Yet somehow, NASCAR's first family has remained strong and free from those vices, and as a result, NASCAR has remained equally strong.

As a family business, NASCAR is run with the same all-American values that you'll find at a local mom-and-pop store. Those values, coupled with a strong family core and business know-how, have made for one of the most successful family businesses in the United States. NASCAR is the only American sport that hasn't had a work stoppage. Hockey, football, basketball and baseball – all our other favorite American pastimes – have, at one point or another, all suffered stoppages. NASCAR never has. The workers haven't unionized as they have in other sports, because they feel they don't need to. NASCAR takes care of its own.

When comparing NASCAR to other sports and businesses in the United States, it becomes clear that we need more family-run operations that are guided, not only by a desire to succeed, but by all-American values. When you drive around the country and come across a mom-and-pop store, you feel good about American business. We need more of those ventures – family-run groceries, restaurants, shops, and delis. When you know that your local businesses share the same values you do, you feel safer. Your family is more secure, and so is the country. You know that the next generation has a work ethic and a business that they will inherit when the time comes. That's what NASCAR is. It's a family business that, thanks to hard work and loyal supporters, was able to grow into the American sports empire that it is today.

Nonetheless, NASCAR does have its problems and challenges, just like any other American business. As it modernizes, it has to find a way to keep its loyal supporters while also meeting the demands and interests of a new generation. The organization has to make tough decisions, like whether or not to keep small tracks in old towns in the South or build bigger tracks outside of other U.S. cities. NASCAR has to perpetuate a modern image while remaining true to its traditional and conservative values. It's an ongoing balance that requires constant dedication, commitment, and creativity.

Yet as time goes on, NASCAR manages to find that balance and attract droves of new fans. Both the people I work with and people in the sports world in general who haven't had exposure to NASCAR keep saying they not only want but *need* to know more about it. That's exactly how I felt before I started broadcasting for the sport. Some new fans are afraid of getting into the sport because they don't know anything about it. NASCAR is a community, and some feel that because they didn't grow up in it or don't know anything about it, they can't be a part of it. I'm proof that the opposite is true. I'm a sports broadcaster for NASCAR, and *I* didn't grow up around it. If you're willing to invest a little bit of time and energy and introduce yourself to the sport, going to a race, watching a broadcast, and having a couple of conversations, you'll love NASCAR.

You'll love the NASCAR community. It's a different kind of sport, so it takes some time to get to know. It's part man, part machine; not two athletes on a field. NASCAR is formatted differently than other sports, but if fans are willing to learn about the drivers, the layout of the sport, and the culture, and if they're willing to talk to other fans about the sport, they'll find a passionate new community.

NASCAR attracts all generations of fans. It really does draw the whole family to the races. Families bring their motor homes and turn a NASCAR event into a vacation. If the kids want to play outside and Mom wants to watch the race, no problem. It's a way to get the whole family involved in a sport, yet everybody gets to do what they're interested in. NASCAR values their fans highly and accommodates them.

When scheduling, most of their races are held on the weekends during the daytime. NASCAR provides the perfect Sunday afternoon for working people. They can come home after church (or sink into the couch after sleeping in), grab something to eat or drink, swipe the remote, and settle in for a couple hours of well-deserved quality entertainment.

Occasionally NASCAR will mix it up and have some races on a Saturday night, such as Bristol's popular night race; however, they do take families into consideration. And it's not just a matter of scheduling – they also give their fans privileges that other sports would never consider, such as allowing them in the pits. It's like standing around the batting cage or being on the field before a game. Those are the types of things that get more people into the sport.

Letting people into the pits and having campgrounds outside the track sets NASCAR apart as a family-oriented sport that is dedicated to its fans. Parents can take their children down to pit road and see their eyes grow wide as they watch their role models and heroes prep for the race. They see up-close the same cars that they buy little toy replicas of. When they get home, they'll tell their friends, "I was there. I saw Dale Earnhardt Jr. talk to his crew chief. I was able to stand really close to his car and get my photograph with it." That's memorable. It's something those kids will never forget.

After an experience like that, those children will remain life-long fans. They'll take their kids to the races to see a whole new generation of drivers. Their children will witness the lightning speed of the cars, just as they did. Though the cars will no doubt be faster and more technologically advanced than the cars from twenty years before, they'll still remind those grown-up children of the very same cars *they* saw when their parents brought them to the races years and years ago. It's a legacy that will never die. And that's what makes NASCAR an American tradition.

9

PAGEANTRY

Sometimes, I'll go to the track very early before anyone gets there. In the silence, I can pause and reflect. I can admire the still beauty of the track. Even as a sports broadcaster, someone whose job it is to talk, I have to admit that the stillness and silence of a normally noisy, wild race track can inspire awe. The steel barriers, the looming lights above the track, the expansive stands, the long stretch of the concrete and asphalt – all combine to form a metal microcosm.

The unyielding architecture and solid metal materials used to create a race track profuse masculinity. It is a modern gladiator's coliseum, a boxer's ring, an adventurer's Everest; it is something to be conquered and something that can conquer you. It has seen victories, but many more defeats. It has seen flames, destruction, and the glory of those who step from crashes and catastrophes unscathed.

Then the stands begin to fill. The camera crew arrives. The teams and drivers begin getting their vehicles ready. A place that was once so austere fills with revving engines and cheering masses.

Everything that is NASCAR inspires wonder – the track, the cars, the crowds, the drivers, and the teams. There's a pageantry to it all that makes every race seem like the Fourth of July. It's a time of simultaneous reflection and sometimes overwhelming celebration.

It's not just a race – it's a carnival, a festival, a family campground, and a neighborhood barbeque. At times it's a patriotic and spiritual event, and sometimes it feels like a celebratory frat party. T-shirts and merchandise fly off the concession stands as people munch on hot dogs and burgers. There are thousands of people there, but it feels like home. No place except the races can feel so big and yet so intimate. When you get to the track, everybody's uniformed heroes are jumping into their bright vehicles. Everyone finds something to be excited about. The drivers feed off of the enormous crowd's energy. Other sports may need cheerleaders, but NASCAR has its fans.

One of my favorite parts is when all the pre-race pageantry is at its climax – the anthem has been sung, the preparations have been completed, and the anticipation of the crowd is at fever pitch. The cars are all lined up. The drivers are gripping their steering wheels. Out of the loud speakers, a voice hollers, "Gentlemen, start your engines!" It's all part of the show. It's a phrase that has been said time and time again, yet never seems to get old. Each time is different, even if the words are always the same.

Another part of the race's pageantry that I love is the national anthem. Despite having heard it many times in other arenas, at the races it always seems more resonant. It could be the band playing or the old trumpet wailing away. Maybe it's everything that our country has been through in the last few years. Or perhaps it's the simple fact that I'm at a race, free and able to enjoy the grandeur of it all. Somehow, when there are fighter planes zooming overhead and you know a good percentage of the audience is tied to the military, the feeling of reverence and loyalty to this country beats strong inside you. It's a time to pause and reflect, but more than anything, it's a time to be proud and admire what this country is capable of. The technology, the cars, the drivers, the patriotic fans – it's a spectacle of which any American can be proud.

The races on D-Day show patriotic NASCAR pageantry at its best as we honor the survivors of Normandy, the men who led the Allies to victory on the shores of France, pushed the Nazi forces into retreat, and conquered Hitler before Paris was set ablaze. On June 6, 1944, there were more than 10,000 casualties, but our proud veterans are still here today. They come on that same fateful day, years later, to honor NASCAR fans and drivers with their presence at the races. On one particularly memorable D-Day, my father was the one to say, "Gentleman, start your engines!" I'll always remember the immense pride I felt when he said those words. The NASCAR industry also marked the tenth anniversary of 9/11 in 2011 during the September race weekend at Richmond International Raceway in Virginia.

The pageantry is more than mere spectacle; it's about being American and patriotic. Regardless of what the calendar says, July 4th, D-Day, Memorial Day, NASCAR makes a point to honor this country. The fans are what make the sport. Since so many fans are highly patriotic or tied to the military in some way, national pride is never far away. The sport honors tradition, and no matter how many times the anthem is played, it will never get old for these crowds.

NASCAR makes patriotism a part of its pageantry.

In many other sports, the anthem isn't televised each time it's played, but in NASCAR they know that fans at home want to hear the anthem. There's something very old-fashioned about NASCAR's pageantry. The start of the race with the announcer's booming voice, the anthem, fans standing in reverence – NASCAR may be one of the most modern and technologically driven sports in the United States, but it's also one of the most traditional.

While NASCAR does have a flair for the dramatic, it doesn't mean making a show of your patriotism. Sometimes saying the anthem can feel more like a chore or going through the motions at some sporting events, but when I'm at a race, it's different. It's one of the reasons why you go: because you feel like you're a part of something bigger. Everyone there is very proud to be American and proud of America as a country. These are your supporters, your fellow countrymen.

That's what makes the anthem so special at a NASCAR race. NASCAR doesn't show the anthem each time for the sake of televising it; on the contrary, it costs them valuable commercial time. Yet, NASCAR makes that sacrifice because their fans want to hear it, as do the drivers, the teams, and all of us in the "Hollywood Hotel" (the portable studio we use for the pre-race coverage) or the broadcast booth. NASCAR doesn't make a show of their patriotism; they let it show.

Of course the rubber-burning, car-crashing spectacle of NASCAR isn't all about patriotism and old-fashioned racing traditions. This is a 180 miles per hour, steel and concrete, cutting-edge sport that attracts speed demons and old timers alike – not to mention old timers who are speed demons. There are even some aspects of NASCAR's pageantry that ruffle a few dusty feathers of the sport's more conservative fans. The adrenaline and high energy rock acts shredding the strings of their guitars on the race track may make some older fans turn off their hearing aids, but many fans love the excitement. And the sight of models such as Pamela Anderson showcased beside NASCAR's finest vehicles make for the perfect combination of sex appeal and horsepower. They can get racy at the races. Yet they tend to tone it down for the sake of families.

Music is becoming a bigger part of the races, and NASCAR is finding ways to get everybody's toes tapping. At Daytona they've had acts from the sixties to today, further proof that many different generations love the sport. It shows the progress that NASCAR has made and all the decades that have come and gone since its introduction into the sports world. Started on dirt roads years ago, it has now grown into a sport with its own traditions and spectacular, larger-than-life racing events.

That's not to say that NASCAR made it completely

on its own. NASCAR didn't grow in a vacuum. It is a part of the American sports dialogue. There are certain traditions that it shares with all other great American sports, such as the national anthem. NASCAR continues to take inspiration from other sports as it decides how it can improve as a form of entertainment. One of the sports it looks toward is football. The NFL has been a role model, in many ways, for NASCAR. From a television standpoint, the NFL is well managed. NASCAR followed suit and is now working with FOX and other national networks. That was a smart decision, because now they have a better way of reaching a large number of people and the affiliation of a major network. The new changes that have been introduced to the sport have really been for the best from an entertainment perspective.

Another way in which NASCAR is modeling itself after other American sports is in the spectacle of the show itself. The Super Bowl is the mother of all televised sporting events and there is no American that isn't familiar with the championship game. Our country's best musicians have performed during the pregame and half-time shows; it is the most watched American television broadcast and Super Bowl Sunday is a de facto holiday. Nobody does a better job with a major sporting event than the NFL and the Super Bowl. So it's no wonder that NASCAR and track officials have been taking notes, adding musicians and more pomp to the races. The Daytona 500 is now referred to as the Super Bowl of racing, but it's quickly becoming an American tradition in its own right.

The Daytona 500 is the Great American Race. The 500-mile, 200-lap race is the pinnacle of the NASCAR Sprint Cup Series. It is the race that determines a driver's greatness. Held on the 2.5-mile tri-oval track in sunny Daytona Beach, Florida, the Daytona 500 is always eventful. It has seen everything from unexpected victories to brawls between drivers. There's always something to see. A lot is at stake; Daytona carries the largest purse of all the races. It is the most watched race and one of the most peculiar competitions in the sports world. Most sports have their major competitions at the end of their seasons, but this race is at the beginning. The Daytona 500 may seem like an unconventional Super Bowl alternative, but it has been around longer than the Super Bowl itself and is becoming just as popular.

Like the Super Bowl, the Daytona 500 has its own traditions. The winning driver is presented with a trophy in Victory Lane. The first Daytona 500 was held in 1959, at the very same place it is held today. Today, a few things have changed, but the race stays true to tradition. Teams have to race in order to set the starting grid. The event is the pinnacle of Speedweeks, two weeks of racing that includes the

Budweiser Shootout and two 150-mile races, which are held on the Thursday before the big race.

With all its pomp and excitement, the Daytona 500 has seen great wins and suffered great losses. Its first winner was Lee Petty, father of NASCAR's arguably greatest driver, Richard Petty, who took the win a record seven times. This jubilant race, for me, also holds an ironic sadness to it; since it is also the race where Dale Earnhardt wrecked in 2001 and died as a result of the accident. The same track that has borne both greatness and tragedy has seen the unexpected victories of underdogs, such as Bobby Allison's win 1978 win. Allison was trailing behind – *way* behind – in thirty-third place. Then, as if by magic, he blasted through the competition and ended up leading by lap 72 of 200. It was the biggest comeback at that time.

But one of NASCAR's most popular races came the next year. If we're going to talk about the show and spectacle of the Daytona 500, we have to talk about the 1979 race that put NASCAR on the map. Perhaps the 1979 race isn't the best example of the all-American sportsmanship that NASCAR seeks to embody, but was certainly historic. It became one of the first races that people really talked about on a national level. It was also the first Daytona 500 to be televised live in its entirety. As fate would have it, a huge snowstorm was covering most of the eastern United States, confining many Americans in their homes with television as a primary means of enter-tainment. That means that most of America saw the entire race, from beginning to finish – and there was a lot to see.

The multi-championship winning Richard Petty stole the win once again, so there was no surprise there. The thing that got everybody talking was what happened *after* the race. On the very last lap, Cale Yarborough and Donnie Allison were head to head, competing for first and the generous purse that accompanied the fame and glory. On the backstretch, the two drivers edged in front of one another, com-peting for the lead – until something went wrong. Yarborough and Allison crashed in turn three, and Petty swooped in to steal first. Yarborough and Allison walked away unharmed . . . or at least, they got out of their *cars* unharmed. Angry after a stolen victory, Yarborough and Allison got into NASCAR's first nationally televised brawl. Donnie's brother, Bobby, stopped to help him out when the fight erupted. It wasn't NASCAR's most honorable moment, but it was certainly one of its most popu-lar. Yes, the spectacle of the Daytona 500 has seen great losses, crushing defeats, and even fistfights.

People are drawn to the races to see more than cars. The Daytona 500 attracts some of the most sought-after celebrities and performers in the country. The pageantry and the pomp are high. Everyone from

Keith Urban, a native New Zealander, to the U.S. Air Force Thunderbird squadron has made a debut at the Daytona 500. Between hearing Urban sing his heart out and watching fighter pilots perform a traditional military flyover, fans who are able to get to Daytona quickly realize that this event is just as big as the Super Bowl. Though it may have less hype, NASCAR has made the great race one of America's greatest sporting events.

Daytona attracts masses of fans, and those that can't make their way to the race set aside the day to watch it on TV. Just like many fans put aside time to enjoy the Super Bowl, NASCAR fans have made the Daytona 500 a national holiday. They invite their friends and families over, prep the recliner and couches, order pizza and buffalo wings, and make it a Daytona 500 Day. The event has earned its own title in the sports world, not as the Super Bowl of NASCAR, but as a premier sporting event in America.

Even though the Daytona 500 is the sport's greatest race, NASCAR makes each of its races a show of pageantry and American pride. Patriotism is never lacking at the races; neither are fast cars, campgrounds, motor homes, barbeques, foods of all varieties, and thousands of the world's most rambunctious fans. The colors of the cars and the sounds of the engines are enough to get these fans on their feet. The crowd makes the race. Everyone is pumped; they create a high-energy atmosphere that makes the event exhilarating. The drivers arguing with the crew chiefs and fans booing their favorite driver's competition are all a part of the spectacle.

Sure, a NASCAR Sprint Cup Series points race may take place thirty-six weeks a year, but some fans see it as the only time when they can let loose. They work hard all week and look forward to the race on the weekend. They're filled with energy that they don't get to express from behind their desks or on the shop floor. They're ready for speed and glory. The fans bring every race to life.

Whether it's football or Formula 1, every sport has pre-game activities, but none compare to that of NASCAR. The fans are really the source of all the commotion during the festivities, camping out days in advance. To them, the race is really just one part of a major party. They go around to vendors as if they were at a carnival and buy collectibles of their favorite drivers. There are hundreds and hundreds of cars, and even more people filling the parking lot. Everyone is there to meet each other, have fun, get their adrenaline pumping – and eat. With countless portable grills and vendors, no one goes hungry at the NASCAR races.

Food isn't the only thing that will catch your eye at the race; you'll see a lot of shining medals and uniforms, too. Some of our military's finest attend the races, and they both give the honor and have the honor of mingling with NASCAR drivers and fans alike. Before the race, drivers will parade around the track for the fans to see them. Before or after this, there will be a performance of either local or national talent. Then, after all the hubbub, the real NASCAR pageantry beings.

Military officials present the American flag. Drivers and team members remove their hats in reverence to pray and sing along to the national anthem. There may be some dispute in this age of political correctness as far as whether public prayer should be allowed at a sporting event. These fans, for the most part, are not only comfortable with praying before a race: many of them would insist upon it. It's a demonstration of personal and communal reverence. Prayer before a race is part of NASCAR's pageantry. It's their way of asking God to watch over the races and make sure that everybody gets to the finish line safe and sound.

The person praying for the group will do nothing more than ask for good weather from the heavens, protection for our drivers at home and our military abroad, and a great race. I think everybody can say "Amen" to that. It isn't that NASCAR doesn't respect the different religious perspectives of its fans – far from it. In truth, the prayer is included precisely because they *do* respect them. NASCAR makes prayer a part of its races because so many of its fans want and expect it to be part of the pre-race pageantry.

After the prayer comes the national anthem. After that, military planes fly over the track like metal angels to bestow their blessings and to prepare every fan and driver alike for the show of glorious man-made, aerodynamically engineered automobiles to come. Then, those famous words, "Gentlemen, start your engines!," and the great green flag. If fans got a chance to go to a pre-game show for baseball, football, hockey, Formula 1, or any other sport in the world, and then rated that experience against the NASCAR pre-game show, there would be no contest: NASCAR would emerge as the undisputed victor.

Many people may wonder how all this began; if NASCAR created all of these elements of the race unprompted, or if fans asked for them. It is, after all, a race, as well as a great sporting event and spectacular show. It's hard to say how it came together to be what it is today, though fans are really the ones to thank for the show. All the patriotism that we see and hear at the races – the military men and women, the planes flying over head, and the sweetly sung American anthem – are ultimately there because fans have, over the years, made the races a place where they can be proud to be American. In fact, they've made a fantastic show of it.

The military men and women are oftentimes big fans themselves and are there to enjoy the race – don't let their uniforms fool you. As for the vendors and merchandise sellers, they're part of most U.S. sporting events; business will go where the customers are. The campgrounds, barbeques, and family-oriented atmosphere have more to do with the fans than with anything else. A lot of NASCAR fans are country-loving folks, the type of people who appreciate the great outdoors and wouldn't dream of going to a fancy hotel with their family when they could take their motor home instead. Maybe, in the early days, this started when a couple of people heard about the races, decided to make a weekend of it, and hopped in their motor homes. It's not hard to believe that it quickly became a popular idea. Over time, these traditions have become what we know today as NASCAR's pre-race celebrations.

The pre-race pageantry is what a lot of the fans come to the races for. Some tradition-oriented fans prefer the sound of country bluegrass over modern rock music. For them the races may get a bit too rowdy at times, but for others, it's that exact excitement that draws them to the event. As in so many other areas, NASCAR has to strike a balance.

In the past it was easier for fans to see the drivers and their teams before they got out on the track. This really added something special for fans going to the races. Fans still have opportunities to see their favorite drivers and teams, but they're limited on race days when crew chiefs are too busy working in the garage and the drivers are most likely with their families in a separate area preparing for the race. Even though their time is often filled with race prep and sponsor obligations, the NASCAR drivers and crews are renowned for their accessibility to their fans in general.

If you really want a good show, access to the crew chiefs, detailed commentary on car technology and race strategy, and an overall deeper and fuller inside look, you need a good sports broadcast. Some fans have access to the teams, the garage area, and the pits through tours and different types of credentials where they are able to converse with the crew members. For all the other fans who don't make it this far, sports broadcasts fill in the gaps by showing them what they can't see. For example, our pit reporters can catch the crew chief and driver talking after a crash. The driver will say, "He came out of nowhere," or, "I don't know what happened." Later, we'll show him the replay and he'll say, "Oh, that was me," and he may even apologize to the other driver. The broadcast is another show and has pageantry itself. From our graphics, to the energy and commentary the announcers bring to the race, to the full-track camera coverage that our broadcast provides, we take our fans to the race and make sure they don't miss a rubber-burning second of it.

My brothers might disagree with me. They were always in the stands at the races. They'd be the first to say that experiencing a race at home on the couch isn't nearly the same as experiencing it at the race track. They'd point out that fans at the races can listen to crew chief-driver radio transmissions just like fans at home, except they can tune into whichever team they want. They may switch to the driver in the lead, and then back to their favorite driver to see how he's doing. If you're on the track, you may not have the benefit of instant replay, but you have the real sound of the cars zooming by, and the smell of the gasoline and all the other industrial fumes that induce a hazy wonder and awe that can only be experienced live.

I'll give it to my brothers: the thrill of seeing a race up close and personal is impossible to recreate, not to mention the excitement of the pre-race show and atmosphere. Fans can say, "I was there. I saw it happen!" It's an unforgettable life experience. However, going to the races in person every week simply isn't a reality for most NASCAR fans. That's why we make the race real on FOX. Through replay, fans are able to analyze the race even before people on the track have a good sense of why a driver crashed or how someone was able to steal the win. We get the best footage and put cameras in every corner. Fans at home get to see the race from every possible angle.

It can also be nice to be at home during inclement weather. Rain, humidity, heat, and cold can't push away the most loyal fan, but it's a lot easier to enjoy the race if you can enjoy the weather, too. At home, these concerns don't apply. However, come rain or shine, the fans do show up with dedication week after week. They are a vital part of the pageantry, standing and cheering each time their drivers race by and singing along to the national anthem. It's these fans who make the sport. It may be an un-choreographed part of the show, but it's the most important.

But before the fans fill the stands, when everyone is still on the road or barbequing at their motor homes, in the moments when I arrive early and revel in the calm before the storm, the track is relatively empty. The teams are off in the garage, and the track, in all its greatness, filled with steel, asphalt or concrete, and history, unfolds before me. I wait for the planes to fly overhead once again and for the air to fill, first with the solemn, sweet sound of the national anthem, then with the uproarious cheer of the crowd and the hearty revving of engines. Those are the sounds of the spectacle that still has the power to take my breath away.

No matter how modern the sport becomes, there are some things that will never change. The vendors will never run out of food, the grills at the campground barbeques will never go cold, and somewhere in America, a race track official will grip a green flag as a robust voice calls out, "Gentlemen, start your engines!" The pageantry, the wonder, and the awe that accompanies every race will always be right there, waiting.

10

HEROES

Who are the real heroes in America?

Ask different people and you'll get different answers. But if we describe a hero as a person with commitment, steadfast dedication, and unfailing courage, I think we'd agree that the real American heroes are the farmers, mechanics, teachers, and everyday people who keep our country strong. They're the ones who work for the greater good – the ones who, although they deserve more praise and more pay, are willing to go to work every day and make this country the great place that it is.

And yet, as we all know, these people aren't typically the first to spring to mind when we think of the word *hero*. It's far more likely that the word conjures up images of stars like Michael Jordan or Jeff Gordon. Why are we more likely to attribute heroism to pro athletes and other people we've put on a pedestal in our society?

The reason is simple: because they make our impossible possible. Pushing the human body and mind to its farthest limits, these heroes show us the greatness of which we are all capable.

NASCAR drivers, sitting behind the wheel of some of the country's fastest, most capable vehicles, with sharp minds and uncanny reflexes, are literally unstoppable. What woman wouldn't want to get in the passenger seat beside these men and drive away from everything? Together, nothing could stop them. One second they're at the office drowning in papers or at home up to their elbows in dishes and busy with the kids, and the next second they're sitting beside a NASCAR driver, speeding down the open road, windows down, with the wind blowing in their hair.

No, these aren't my fantasies. They're the daydreams of a few of the female sports fans who have been bold enough to fill me in on who their sports heroes are and what draws them to these NASCAR drivers. They've told me they like the tough-yet-touchable look these drivers have. They often compare them to firemen. It's no wonder – with their gear and uniform, they look like they could easily burst through the door of a house on fire. Their uniforms are, in fact, fireproof.

NASCAR attracts a certain kind of driver. Imagine a quintessential NASCAR driver, like Richard Petty or Dale Earnhardt – essentially John Wayne on wheels. The car comes tearing down the track with full force. It stops, twirling in a half circle, steam rising from the asphalt. An arm appears through the open driver's side window, followed by a helmet and the rest of the body contorting itself to maneuver through the small opening, and out from the mist steps a superhero-like figure dressed in full uniform. The figure approaches, almost in slow motion. It removes its helmet to reveal . . . long, flowing, soft hair, and a sweet smile.

Wasn't quite what you were expecting, right? This image is, of course, contrary to the John Wayne–on-wheels image for which NASCAR has become known. Yet women are making their way into the sport. While women have never been hindered or denied entrance, drivers in NASCAR's circuits have predominately been men. The sport hasn't seen many successful female drivers. Even so, it would be good to see more women on the track. People in the sport may very well be thrown off by an increase in female participation, a change that wouldn't come without a few raised eyebrows, but a female driver has the ability to bring more female fans to the sport. She would also serve as a good role model for young girls interested in NASCAR.

However, to find a talented female driver is difficult. The latest candidate people look toward now is Danica Patrick. She was named Rookie of the Year in the IndyCar Series, was the first woman to win an Indy car race, and has brought a wider awareness to open-wheel racing. Certainly these are notable achievements. There are skeptics who say that although she has accomplished a great deal, the reason why she gets as much attention as she does is simply because she is a woman.

But Patrick wouldn't be out there if she couldn't drive. Yes, she happens to have sex appeal and is maximizing her career. With all the commercials and shoots she does, she is getting very profitable publicity. But that doesn't in any way negate the fact that she is one of the first women to break into racing, which has remained a man's sport for years. Her work up to this point has been very praiseworthy. Whatever the case, now that she has raced a few races in the NASCAR Nationwide Series with JR Motorsports, I'm interested to see what she can accomplish over her next few seasons in NASCAR. NASCAR has had female drivers in the past, but they haven't been able to compete regularly on a high level. If she's serious about NASCAR as a sport and devoted to it, despite her recent struggles in the NASCAR Nationwide Series, I wouldn't be surprised to see Danica Patrick leading the pack one day. As she prepares to compete in ten races in the 2012 NASCAR Sprint Cup Series season in a car fielded by Stewart-Haas Racing, she could very well be at the top of the pack this coming year.

As much as NASCAR is a family-like community, it remains old-fashioned in many respects. With that family-oriented, down-to-earth, southern mentality comes an outlook that can be starkly conservative. Having more female role models like Patrick behind the wheel makes for a positive and refreshing change. The driver's seat is definitely the most visible spot in the sport, but it isn't the only place where women can start getting involved in NASCAR. Before Patrick became so popular, women had already been involved in different aspects of racing for years. Lesa France Kennedy is the chairman of International Speedway Corporation (ISC), which operates twelve of the tracks on which NASCAR's premier series races. There are women in all departments within NASCAR, and women at the track in capacities other than driving. Today, you'll see female officials and women pit-crew members working alongside men. They're still a minority, but the door is open, and in fact,

NASCAR is working hard on diversity programs. We've reached a point in American society – and NASCAR reflects that – where performance is what matters, not social categories.

NASCAR is about celebrating values like teamwork, courage, self-sacrifice, toughness, precision, skill, devotion, and good old-fashioned hard work – and none of those values are gender based. Anyone can join the club. No one's going to be interested in whether you're a man or a woman; they're going to be interested in whether or not you can get the job done. This is a sport that has some tough moments for everybody, from economic constraints to constant travel to working under extreme stress and in dangerous conditions. If you can handle that, you're in, no matter your race, creed, religion – or gender.

The great thing about NASCAR's diversity efforts is that they're extending into the sport's positive influence on children. It's a newer trend, so there aren't a lot of official statistics yet, but I can say for sure from my own observation that girls and young women are getting involved in go-karting in much higher numbers than in the past. Girls are feeling much more comfortable putting on a helmet and jumping behind the wheel. They're right there alongside boys learning all the extraordinary skills and values the sport has to offer. And whether or not they stay in it through the professional level isn't important – the real benefit is that they'll carry what they learned into their lives and careers and families as they grow up. They've got a role model in Danica Patrick and in the many other women of racing – in NASCAR and in open-wheel, on the track and in support roles – and that's going to be a positive influence no matter what they decide to do with their lives.

Women aren't the only focus of NASCAR's search for new talent and fans right now. NASCAR is going after the younger generation, with younger fans who are attracted to younger drivers. While young fans are important, there are fans of all ages interested in the sport. Youth needs to be balanced with maturity, experience, and age. One of NASCAR's unique draws is that it's a sport for all ages, and if they focus too heavily on just the younger fans and drivers, they risk losing that advantage. Some of the greatest NASCAR heroes have been well into their prime when they really made their mark.

Jimmie Johnson won five straight NASCAR Sprint Cup Series championships, an accomplishment unparalleled in NASCAR history. He was the first NASCAR driver to be voted Associated Press Male Athlete of the Year. As someone who has covered great runs like the New England Patriots in the Super Bowl or Phil Jackson's NBA coaching career, I consider Johnson's record, along with his crew, one of the greatest accomplishments in the history of sports. Johnson has won the NASCAR Sprint Cup titles in a variety of ways, including carrying a points lead into the Chase for the NASCAR Sprint Cup and also coming back from a deficit. Very impressive driving, to say the least.

At FOX Sports, to honor Johnson on our pre-race show, we interviewed some of the great athletes whose careers included great winning runs. These included Derek Jeter of the New York Yankees, hockey's Wayne Gretzky, and seven-time Tour de France winner Lance Armstrong. Gretzky had a beautiful comment. He said that what Johnson has done "is truly an amazing accomplishment. Jimmie, you truly are the Great One!"

One of Johnson's biggest fans is Armstrong, who had nothing but praise for the driver's run. In fact, after the Armstrong interview aired, Johnson called him for advice about how to keep his streak alive. The cyclist's guidance, from one long-enduring champion to another: stay hungry. Keep doing more. Even if you're just as good from one year to the next, your competition will be better, and more people will be gunning for you. Know your own limitations and restrictions, but don't allow yourself to be mentally or physically complacent. Wise advice, don't you think?

Jimmie Johnson came from humble beginnings. He was not a "ticketed superstar" for whom great things were predicted. Early in his career, he was just another driver looking for a chance to succeed. Jeff Gordon spotted Johnson's talent and got him a ride, but he made his own success.

Like Gordon, he's a California kid. Johnson is one of the most humble athletes ever to achieve success at the highest levels in sport. He's down to earth and never gets carried away with himself. Yet he's one of the least appreciated champions in the sport. Fans respect how he handles himself and who he is, and tries to be.

You could compare Johnson to tennis star Pete Sampras – a champion with no marital problems, one who doesn't make the headlines for trouble with the law or having a reputation for staying out drinking. Johnson once told me he was a little bit of a class clown growing up in El Cajon, in southern California, but he learned to play by the rules. He is by no means an outsider in NASCAR, having succeeded at the highest levels, but maybe he lacks that "bad-boy" attitude that resonates with some fans.

By contrast, you've got Tony Stewart who, in 2011, enjoyed the greatest comeback in the history of the Chase. He hadn't won a race all year prior to the Chase and then won five out of ten events to overtake Carl Edwards in the last race of the year at Homestead-Miami Speedway. Stewart had already won two championships, but 2011 was his first as an owner-driver. Some people call him polarizing: he's charitable but also brash, with a tendency to "tell it like it is." He won't back down, either in a conversation or on the race track. Is he more relatable to NASCAR fans? Depends on whom you ask.

When it comes to finding heroes in NASCAR, you don't have to look far – and I mean that quite literally. The heroic drivers who keep fans tuning in week after week could just as easily be your neighbors; in fact they very well may be. NASCAR is a different kind of sport, one in which the players are real Americans. I don't weigh 300 pounds, I can't get out on a field and tackle goliath-like men, and I can't hit a 93-mile-per-hour fast ball – but I can drive. Our country's car culture is what makes NASCAR the real American sport. The car is the great equalizer. It gives every driver a chance. Whether fans are in the car, on their way to work, getting their license for the first time, or just being a kid riding around in go karts, they can connect to the sport. It's more than just a fantasy; it's something you do every day.

Fans can relate to racing, yet at the same time, they may not want to find themselves going close to 180 miles per hour on a curving speedway for hundreds of miles with forty-two other cars surrounding them. They respect the skill that it takes to be part of the sport, but they let someone else take the risks. They can relate to it and understand it at a basic level, and they admire NASCAR drivers for going beyond it.

Being able to relate to the sport and the drivers is what makes NASCAR everyone's sport. We would be losing something by making the sport less amicable toward female drivers and fans, or making it a sport that solely targets younger people. I'd like to believe that no matter how much change the sport sees, it will always remain the NASCAR that it has been for decades. It is my hope that Dale Earnhardt, Richard Petty, and all the other all-American tough guys who embody the image of the NASCAR star driver will never lose their place on the track, even if the time has come for them to start sharing it with new and diverse faces.

If this chapter is about heroes and NASCAR, there are some drivers who cannot go unmentioned, drivers who have made the sport what it is today. That list starts with Richard Petty, who is the most successful NASCAR driver in history. He has seven Daytona 500 victories and seven NASCAR premier series titles to his name and saw his glory days in the 1960s and 1970s. And there's Dale Earnhardt, of course – one of NASCAR's greatest heroes. Having won seventy-six races in his time and seven NASCAR premier series titles, there's no telling what he could have done if he stayed on the track. The Waltrip brothers and the Earnhardt family have racing in their blood; those families, like many NASCAR families, seem to have sports hero genes. Still more, there's

Bobby Allison who was an aggressive driver who conquered all at three Daytona 500s, his brother Donnie Allison, who picked up two wins at Talladega, and his son, Davey Allison, who won his first NASCAR premier series race at Talladega Superspeedway in 1987 and came away with the Rookie of the Year Award that same year.

We've mentioned Cale Yarborough, but he did a lot more than brawl during his time in NASCAR. He won the Daytona 500 four times and took home three NASCAR Sprint premier series championships *in a row*. A.J. Foyt is another race car driver for the history books. He raced everything from dirt-track to sports cars. He wasn't only a four-time winner of the Indy 500; he also sped into Victory Lane at the Daytona 500.

And it's hard to say NASCAR without hearing the name Jeff Gordon. A child prodigy, Gordon started racing when he was five. He's got trophies from nearly every NASCAR race – from the Coca-Cola 600 to the Daytona 500.

It's hard to say what makes a NASCAR hero what they are. It has a lot to do with talent, speed, and a certain confidence, but how these men got from the highway to the race track and what direction they went in to get there is difficult to say. Every story is different. I happen to think it boils down to a combination of luck, determination, and great talent. Unlike other sports, in NASCAR, that can be enough.

The drivers in NASCAR don't have to fit into a certain physical mold to participate in the sport.

Mark Martin is an excellent example of an all-American driver who is mature and experienced. In his sixth decade of life, he may be older than the rest of the pack, but he's better than the majority of the young drivers and rookies on the track. After moving 180 miles per hour for the better part of his life, he had decided, not too long ago, to slow down. Rick Hendrick had to talk him out of early retirement. There are only a limited few capable of doing what he does, and Hendrick Motorsports has really benefited from his experience.

Martin chose to go back to work with Hendrick Motorsports, which is arguably one of the best teams on the track in terms of advertising, expertise, and sponsorship. He's surprised with what he's done because he's accomplished so much this time around. Fans are impressed, too.

Although in 2012 he begins a new career with Michael Waltrip Racing, his popularity remains the same. His image as a mature male driver draws fans to him. He seems reliable and trustworthy. That's what makes him a good role model for young fans and an inspiring peer for drivers and fans alike. If a parent had to pick a sport to draw role models from, NASCAR would be the best choice. It's a sport that is driven by all-American values and that's frankly much cleaner than other sports. The drug issues that officials encounter in NASCAR pale in comparison to other major American sports today. NASCAR drivers, for the most part, simply don't need to go down that path. In terms of performance, there are few drugs they can take that can make their car go faster or make them better drivers. In other sports, athletes go as far as they can go, then they see other athletes getting farther. When they find out the secret to their success, it's not surprising that they seek to further their careers and improve their athletic ability by taking that magic pill. It's a vice, but it's a vice that America shares with its athletes. From health supplements to pharmaceuticals to diet pills, there are millions of Americans looking for a quick fix.

The violations seen in NASCAR are either due to uppers, which drivers may take to stay more alert, or non-performance-enhancing drugs taken recreationally off the track. They include cocaine and methamphetamine, which have a decidedly negative effect on performance as well as general health. If you're using drugs to aid you in other sports, you can be a better player, but in NASCAR they can cause a crash. It's just dangerous, and it puts yourself and other drivers at risk. With safety in mind, NASCAR does and will crack down on all drug use – and nobody's going to stop them. In fact, if NASCAR officials don't stop a driver under the influence, other drivers will.

There's no tolerance for drug use among drivers. They police themselves. It's kind of like they're saying, "Hey man, don't do drugs and get out on the track with me. I'll fight you right here before you get in that car." They're able to keep an eye on each other's behavior. Drivers know each other. Traveling with the same teams and group of people almost year-round really draws drivers together. They compete against each other, but they also work and live together. They're close and know each other's business. While they respect personal privacy and space, this is also a community. If somebody's threatening the group, their behavior needs to be checked.

NASCAR drivers can be tough and old school. They'll say, "I may be taking a risk here, but I don't like what you're doing." Fistfights are common in NASCAR. Officials don't condone the behavior, but among drivers there's an unwritten moral code that they *will* enforce. That's why they sometimes apologize to each other if they foul up during a race and get into somebody else's way. There's a gentlemen's code about competition. It can be downright strange how they'll help each other out, even during a competition, but it's a very healthy competitive atmosphere.

American business had a similar competitive atmosphere years ago, before people became greedy and cutthroat. It used to be, "You're American, I respect what you're doing, let's work together here." Times may have unfortunately changed outside of NASCAR, but these drivers have maintained their sense of sportsmanship. Even the way they compete is honorable. The sportsmanship and healthy competition in NASCAR is something that everyone can learn from, not only in sports, but in American big business. These guys work with and compete against one another the way heroes do.

NASCAR drivers may be speed demons and daredevils with one very tough, aerodynamically engineered exterior, but underneath it all they are guided by strong American values. They remember their roots, and whether they're competing on the track or wearing a three-piece suit talking to sponsors, they never forget who they are. That's what makes NASCAR America's real sport. These drivers, underneath their uniforms and gear, are real Americans. They're more a part of real America than other athletes and celebrities we see on TV today. Even when they reach the top, they don't look down on the rest of America. They may be heroes to their fans, but they're not putting themselves on pedestals.

NASCAR drivers are on the track to race. They're not, however, racing away from anything. Drivers are proud of where they've come from. The culture that many celebrities adhere to involves hitting up clubs and bars, dating and dumping models, and becoming big spenders. For the most part, NASCAR drivers stay away from that celebrity culture. They follow the rules of society – well, for the majority of the time. There is one little problem that a lot of the drivers have when it comes to following the rules. Speeding.

Gordon once told me that NASCAR drivers are the worst kind of people to get stuck in traffic. They hate bad drivers, but even more, they know that they can get where they're going a lot more quickly . . . if only they were able to drive faster and more strategically. They have to make a concerted effort to remember that the world is not a race track. That's the only time they have trouble thinking, "I'm here like everybody else." It's very frustrating for them to be out there and not be able to cut people off.

Yet, off the road, these drivers find themselves at home, the place where their families and communities instilled all those values in the first place – values like patriotism and putting family first. If societal pressure isn't enough to keep these speed demons in line, then NASCAR will do it. The drivers are held responsible for their actions. They live in a world with consequences, just like the rest of us. It's the real world here, and drivers have more at stake. They won't be getting off because they're star drivers. They have to play by the rules of society and the rules of NASCAR, or they won't be playing at all.

NASCAR drivers can oftentimes be hell-raisers and risk-takers, but at the end of the day, they have people to answer to and they have that strong conscience that their families and communities have instilled in them. They know that everyone they love is holding them accountable, and they know that this community, from NASCAR's fans to its officials, doesn't tolerate illicit behavior. In addition, NASCAR's fans and the drivers' families and communities oftentimes come from the working class. They understand the value of a hard-earned dollar. To see their drivers flaunting their wealth on illicit or dangerous activities wouldn't bring them to admire them more; it would make them shake their heads. These fans want heroes with a sense of pride in their country, American values, and talent paired with humility. Those are the things most drivers have that make them the star athletes and role models they are.

However, it is important to remember – not only in NASCAR, but in all sports – that the true heroes are not the athletes and drivers. Certainly there are drivers who are sports heroes; they continuously inspire people to follow their dreams. Yet the true heroes are in the stands. The true heroes are the dads and moms bringing their sons and daughters to the race for the first time. The true heroes are the military men and women who honor NASCAR by attending the races, year after year. Those are the people whom NASCAR honors and respects. In our society, too much emphasis is given to people who make gross amounts of money – they may be rich, but that doesn't make them heroes. There are more heroes in the stands than out there on the track.

When I see kids in the pits looking at the drivers and the cars, I may see wonder in their eyes, but it's not hero worship; it's the car, the colors, the excitement of the track. They're overwhelmed and excited by everything that's going on. These kids are really more interested in the cars and excitement than the drivers themselves. Kids will have a great time with their families at the races and develop a love for the track. They learn to be part of a great community while acquiring an interest in a sport that they'll be able to share with their children. It's not about idolizing heroes – it's about being a part of a community and cultivating a passion for racing that can be shared among generations. The races are a great place for families to spend time together. Kids are more likely to find heroes not on the track, but right beside them in the stands.

Oddly enough, it's the parents and adults who often place the NASCAR drivers on a pedestal. They relate to them and admire them, often because drivers are closer in age to adult fans. A lot of them have families and responsibilities, and they're role models for adults. These drivers aren't raw athletes or meatheads. You probably won't turn on the TV to see one of these drivers standing in his underwear for a commercial. However, you *will* see them spending time with their kids and with their families. It's only once they put on that uniform and get in the car that they turn into action heroes.

Physically, these heroes aren't always what you'd expect. Martin, who is over fifty, actually has a better physique than most drivers because he exercises and eats well. He takes extremely good care of himself and looks great because of it. There is a value placed on physical fitness in NASCAR, but it's not anywhere near as strenuous as it is in other sports. Even physically speaking, these drivers are more similar to their fans. The average driver body type isn't phenomenally different from the average guy on the street. What matters is whether the drivers are skilled or not. Drivers don't have to be the strongest men or have a certain type of body. Nobody is concerned with how much they can bench at the gym or if they've got washboard abs – that's just not a part of the game.

There's something very American about a sport that offers everyone an opportunity to be involved, no matter what they look like. As an equal opportunity sport, it gives everybody hope. Someone who is five foot seven doesn't have to be discouraged from trying the sport. Being small might even help; it may mean that it's easier to fit inside the car comfortably for long hours, adding less weight to the car in general, and overall helping its speed.

After speaking to female fans, I know that many women find drivers attractive for their ability more than their physique. It's the spirit and confidence that these drivers exude on the track that make them sexy. And the male fans relate to drivers. They can see themselves out there in the driver's seat. In America, even the little guy can feel like a big shot behind the wheel. This isn't to say that the men of NASCAR are physically undesirable and are over-compensating. It simply explains the hero fantasy that draws both men and women to these drivers, men who may not have all the physical qualifications that a basketball player has but are hero-worthy in many other ways.

NASCAR drivers are heroes because of who they are, not because of how they look or how much money they have. They're a part of real America. The all-American values that have made this country into what it is today beating strong in the hearts of NASCAR fans and drivers alike. NASCAR is a community. It's a community that honors its fans just as much as its drivers. These drivers may be making millions, but that's not the reason why they're heroes. A respect for country, a moral compass, and talent coupled with humility are what turn a NASCAR driver into an American legend.

Drivers come from backgrounds that have instilled in them values and morals that prevent them from losing touch with who they are and why they're here.

Their gentlemen's code of conduct and healthy sense of competition are noble and heroic. The rest of America, especially American business, could learn a lot from the way these athletes compete. It's not just about competing; it's about racing. Sure, drivers look like superheroes in full gear and uniform; they take risks every time they race and are faster than a speeding bullet. But the true mark of a hero at a NASCAR race isn't in their outfit, their skill, or their paycheck – it's in their heart.

The *real* heroes on the track are the military men and women who come to the track, the hard-working parents who take their family to NASCAR sporting events on the weekends, and the many fans who work to make this country what it is during the week. They may not have the biggest houses or the finest automobiles, but they're the ones who are contributing to American society and making this nation great. Those are the real American heroes, and NASCAR honors them.

11

ENDURANCE

merica is great. Magnificent and almost overwhelmingly large, it is one of the biggest countries in the world. Its diverse landscape stretches from sea to shining sea, from the Appalachian Mountains to the redwood forests, from the plains of South Dakota to the Gulf of Mexico. The varied landscape bears witness to the size and diversity of this nation.

The culture and people are just as varied as

landscape. A Texas steak is very different than a New York rib eye, and a southern home-cooked meal is very different than a South Beach diet dish. At times, depending on the locale, the United States can be traditional to the point of being starkly conservative. In other places in the United States, tradition is quickly traded for advancement and progress.

And, if there is ever doubt as to the America's strength, visit New York and the New York Stock Exchange on Wall Street. These are the people who control America's wealth and money. The energy of the city, the buildings that literally scrape the sky, and the constant flow of suits on Wall Street – they're all still there.

However, over the last several years, this country's financial security has come into question. Suddenly, it's become evident that the money that America invested was being poorly managed. Wall Street is where the money is; it's where it's traded and trans- ferred so that hopefully it can be better invested in the business world. It's there so American business has the resources it needs to compete and continue to run like clockwork. Whether it was laziness, greed, or irresponsibility that caused the economic crisis, it's hard to say. As a country, we are all trying to learn where we went wrong and how we can best manage our resources in order to become better competitors in the future. Our country has not experienced a financial crisis such as this since the Great Depression – this is new for all of us, and we are, as a result, being forced to learn how to endure.

NASCAR is not exempt from the current economic climate. Fortunately, NASCAR has proven itself resilient in times of turmoil. After half a century of success in business, there's a lot that the American business and financial world can learn from NASCAR and the way it has handled itself. There is no test greater than the test of time. NASCAR may be old-fashioned in many respects, but it's these home-grown all-American values that have kept NASCAR on track financially and in the sports world for decades. These values are what our country desperately needs in an era when businesses exchange sustainable practices for short-sighted success. We need business practices that are guided by the morals that have kept NASCAR in business for over sixty years. We need tips, guidance, and an overall strategy for how to *endure*.

NASCAR embodies so much of what the United States is and what it should be. It's a competitive environment, but it's a healthy competitive environment. It's a tradition, but it welcomes techno-logical advancement and progress. It respects its roots and stays down-to-earth, yet is one of the most successful and fastest growing motorsports in the world.

The United States thrives on capitalism and, like NASCAR, needs competition. Without competition, there would be no races and there would be no capitalism. Without capitalism, the U.S. economy would be irrevocably changed. Still, the competitive spirit in the business world has become extreme, showing itself to be corrupt. Between Enron, the Lehman Brothers loan scandal, and the Bernie Madoff Ponzi scheme, the American people have watched helplessly as the financial industry gobbled up their hard-earned money as it pushed ahead. For every scandal America witnesses, we know that there are a dozen more hidden from public view.

In NASCAR, cheating used to be a part of the culture. It was out in the open. With time, NASCAR officials cracked down on violations, and now the sport is one of the best-regulated sports in the United States. Likewise, the American people and the U.S. government have a responsibility to check the power of the financial industry. We need to learn to crack down, NASCAR-style. If the business world was checked in the same way that NASCAR polices its teams and drivers, corruption wouldn't be able to run rampant. Americans and their money would be significantly safer, and we'd all be a lot happier as a result.

In NASCAR, they have a zero-tolerance policy when it comes to issues such as drug use. It's not a violation of rights. If there's a driver whom they suspect is using, they'll say, "We need to test you and we will, because it is a privilege to be a part of NASCAR." That's why there are so few drivers partaking in illicit behavior. I give NASCAR a lot of credit in that department – they're concerned about doing what's right.

NASCAR handles things without pomp and press. The NASCAR executives try to take care of things in a private matter – close to home and behind closed doors. NASCAR handles itself well in tight situations because of the careful way in which they address issues. Whether it's driver drug use or an economic crisis, so far the sport has not seen a storm it cannot weather. I think that's mainly because they always keep two things in mind: their morals and their fans.

The healthy and admirably competitive atmosphere that is found on and off a NASCAR track is all too rare in our day and age. Teams will help each other if one is missing a needed part. I'm sometimes shocked at how helpful they will be. For them, it's not about winning. It's about racing; it's about the sport. Sure, everyone wants to win. But at the end of the day, if that's the only reason you're on the track, you're going to lose motivation. You're going to run out of fuel. It's not just about the finish line or the prize; it's about community.

In the American business world today, so many people only look at numbers and dollar signs. The customer is second to the profit. Businesses are getting larger, less personal, more motivated by money, and less motivated by a desire to serve and be a productive part of a community. NASCAR has been so successful because it isn't solely concerned with profit. It's a sport that grew out of a family, which slowly grew into a much larger community. NASCAR was a small operation that developed, not due to cutthroat business tactics, but because people loved the sport. Today NASCAR is still a community, still a family-run business, and still guided by the all-American values that have kept it strong for over sixty years. This is the secret to how it has endured.

Like many things that endure, NASCAR embodies a strong element of tradition. Gearheads and fans watch the sport ritually every Sunday, go to certain races every year with their families, and make NASCAR a regular part of their lives. Yet although it's a tradition for thousands nationwide, NASCAR isn't necessarily a sport stuck in its ways, and it most certainly isn't a sport stuck in the past. The reason why it has been able to survive through all these years is because it has been able to change with the times. Adaptability is important for survival. NASCAR has grown technologically and economically to better function in a modern world. From taking Toyota on as a sponsor to developing new engineering and safety advancement for their vehicles, NASCAR has proven that it can endure and adapt to the fluctuations of our fast-paced, ever-changing society.

It is this blend – NASCAR's ability to honor tradition while simultaneously advancing as a high-tech sport – that is the secret formula for how the sport has not only endured through tough times, but prospered. No matter how far it goes, it never gets too far ahead of itself. Despite everything, NASCAR respects its roots. The drivers may go from rags to riches, but they don't throw out their rags. The NASCAR community isn't a country club – you don't need money to join (even if you do need it to race). In fact, it'd probably help if you didn't have it and understood what it was to come home to watch a race after a hard week's work. It's a sport that stays down-to-earth, no matter what happens. NASCAR has certainly earned its fortune and bragging rights – it's one of the leading motorsports in the world – but it's determined to stay humble and accessible to its loyal fans. If it loses sight of its fans, it loses everything.

I connect to the NASCAR community in the same way many fans do: because I know what it is to live simply and with limited means. I have a deeply ingrained respect for the hard-working Americans that keep this country running. Even though I'm a successful sports broadcaster now, I came from modest beginnings. My father worked two jobs to support five kids. Life wasn't always easy given our family's economic status, but it would have been even harder if we hadn't been able to rely on each other. It was our love for one another, our commitment to our own little nuclear community that gave us the strength to endure.

In the same way, NASCAR fans have that community. There's a lot our country can learn from that mentality. Even when times get rough and economic resources run thin, the thing to remember is that we still have each other. The intelligence, technology, good morale, and work ethic that built this country up aren't monetary – there's no price tag attached. Those are resources we can still find in each other. To play the blame game, let politics get in the way, or turn on each other would have been the worst thing to do during the economic crisis. It became more about realizing that it was time to work together as a society, rely on each other as a community, and tap into our human resources in order to endure these tough times. The true test of strength does not come when you are at your strongest, but when you are at your weakest. American society is being tested. In order to endure, we have to pull together and work with each other to find sustainable solutions.

My father taught me a lot about enduring economically. His advice isn't anything stretched too far beyond common sense: You save money when you work, and you don't buy something you can't afford.

If you do buy something on credit, like a home or car, you make sure you can make the payments. You have to make sure your investments are worth it to you. Even if you can afford it now, can you keep up with it?

If only our nation had been asking itself those simple questions over the last few years leading up to the recent economic collapse. The fact is we as a country *couldn't* keep up with it. We couldn't keep up with our oil costs and how much we were, and still are, consuming. We're a society that relies on consumption, but we came to a point where we couldn't afford to continue to consume and take. That's why finding straightforward, sustainable solutions was, and still is, important. We have to be honest with ourselves about how many resources we have and how much we are consuming and creating. Our economic problems in the auto and banking industry stemmed from business practices that weren't productive but were actually costing money.

Once again, NASCAR sets a good example: they're very honest about how much money they make and how successful they are. They're a champion of sustainable business operation. They started with a strong base of fans, and they have a regular demand for races, which they fill. When they expanded their business, they didn't grow too fast. As the saying goes, "Don't spread yourself too thin." What was once a southern regional sport has now spread to the entire country, but it didn't happen overnight; they expanded when times were good, waiting until they had the tracks and the audience in regions they were expanding to. It's common sense. Don't spread yourself too thin, and don't spend money if you're not making it. NASCAR has experienced exponential growth because they worked with what they had when they had it, and they grew. Because of their strategy, they have now been able to slowly grow outside of the country and gain exposure and begin series in Canada, Mexico, and Europe.

Though NASCAR has fared well in tough times, it too must tighten its belt during this economic recession. Fans are as loyal as ever, but their wallets may be a bit thinner. Families still come with their motor homes to every race, but as families tighten their spending, their ticket purchases become less frequent. Taking time off from work and paying for the fuel to get to race day are becoming greater burdens. Yet, NASCAR needs its fans. And since its fans are everyday Americans, the sport needs to find a way to still be affordable while trying to survive in the new economic climate.

NASCAR isn't any different than any other businesses or individual in the United States today. We all need to make choices. However, that doesn't mean NASCAR can choose profit over its fans. The fans are the people who got the sport where it is today. That's why NASCAR has to find a way to keep the sport affordable. There are many companies out there that are taking advantage of their "fans" or the people who helped them to grow. Whether the companies are increasing premiums so that they are grossly unaffordable to most of the public, or whether they are imposing mandatory fines, fees, and taxes, they are jeopardizing the support they have received from their customers. But NASCAR plays by a different set of rules. It never forgets the people who make it what it is. In good times and bad, it remains everyone's sport.

American business is suffering, but perhaps it's time to be proactive. It's a lot like a driver in a race. The American people are behind the wheel. They have decisions to make. The car starts out strong, but then things wear down and there are malfunctions. The American business world is malfunctioning. We need to stop what we're doing, access the problem properly, and fix it. It will take valuable time, money, and expertise, but it must be done. We have a choice: we can keep going and either crash or run out of fuel, or we can make that pit stop and fix the problem. Slowing down isn't something American society is used to doing, but it's something we have to do.

It also means we have to consume less. Fans used to go to football games, rock concerts, and NASCAR races. Now they have to make just one choice. It's all a vital life lesson in endurance. People today don't even know how secure their jobs are. They're good at what they do, people like them at work, but sometimes they get cut anyway. Yet, it's our attitudes toward the economy and our determination to find sustainable solutions that will dictate the security of our future. No matter what, we have to keep going.

In order to keep going, we need to pull together – a sentiment that isn't hard to find in NASCAR. Jeff Gordon was the first to say, "I'll take less money to help the sport." He cares about the future of NASCAR, but more so, I think he cares about the fans. He wants NASCAR to be a sport that everyone can be a part of. He also said that he wanted his crew to stay intact. Drivers aren't throwing their teams under the bus. They'll make sacrifices for each other so the community can get through this together. Gordon was the first to grasp how important the NASCAR community is and see the big picture in this crisis.

Dale Earnhardt Jr. may not have a NASCAR Sprint Cup championship, but he's very connected to the fans and to the sport. He's proven himself over the long run as a driver and a part of this community, and he is dedicated to remaining loyal to NASCAR in both the good times and the bad. The words and support of the drivers for the greater NASCAR community are a sign of loyalty and the strong sense of togetherness that will keep the sport strong, even in the most difficult of times.

The organization's way of addressing the economic situation has been interesting. It hasn't just been lawyers and corporate heads talking things over. Instead it's been the France family, the executives, the owners, and the drivers, sitting together and talking about what should be done. There's something admirable about this. In a world of lawyers, corporations, paperwork, and bureaucracy, it's nice to find a sport that puts people who are actually a part of the sport in charge.

Every year, NASCAR reviews the NASCAR Sprint Cup race schedule and often changes the order in which the races occur. One week NASCAR is in the South, a couple weeks later they're in another region, and then they're back in the South just a few weeks after leaving. NASCAR really counts on the opinions of their drivers and owners, and they try to handle all shows and scheduling as a community, listening to everybody's needs, not just the needs of a business.

When there are issues in the sport, financial or otherwise, they can turn to each other for guidance and advice. NASCAR works closely with team owners such as Roger Penske, Joe Gibbs, and Rick Hendrick. They also work with the major corporate sponsors such as Coca-Cola, Office Depot, and Unilever. The sponsors are just as personally invested in the sport as they are financially invested in it and thus are an important part of the NASCAR business.

NASCAR really does value American business, but the sponsors don't run the show. The sport isn't completely controlled by a pull on the pocket or the monetary powers of sponsors. First and foremost, they care about the fans, and they want to make sure that they get the racing they want. Of course NASCAR strives to be modern and cool for the sake of progress and profit, but not at the expense of the sense of tradition or morality that are so important to its fans.

NASCAR is very connected to its fans and everyday Americans. They share those same all-American values, and they also realize the hardship that these families must weather in the current economic climate. There is a connection between what NASCAR is feeling financially and how American society feels. Yet when race day comes and the track fills with fans and the sound of revving engines, bank statements and gloomy financial news forecasts fade away. Even so, a certain amount of apprehension is healthy. As we mature individually and as a society, we pause, reflect, and sometimes worry a bit more about the future generations. We want to ensure that tomorrow will be a brighter day; that we will leave our children a world even better than our own.

The truth is we don't simply want to endure and survive. We want to thrive. What will be our legacy?

We can worry as much as we like, but worrying never got any work done. Our society was, and is considered, by some, to still be, in an economic crisis, energy crisis, and everything else crisis, but we can endure and resolve these issues. However, we won't get it done by saying we can't, or simply by talking about how horrible it is or how hard it will be. Well-thought-out, sustainable, and prepared solutions are feasible – if only we work together to achieve them.

Just like on the race track, there's no such thing as too late, too old, or too hopeless in life. Think of Mark Martin, a man racing past the age of fifty who might as well be twenty. He once told me that worrying is like a rocking chair: if you don't go anywhere, it gives you something to do. American society is going somewhere, but we have to stop sitting in our rocking chairs worrying and start thinking of solutions instead. We need to listen to each other and find a carefully planned, well-informed way to address our current crises. We have the brainpower; it's time to put it to work. Martin had all the driving talent in the world when he retired. When he made his comeback to Hendrick Motorsports, he didn't do it without thought. He made sure he had the best team, the best resources, and the best sponsorship backing him. Even now, as he starts his 2012 career with Michael Waltrip Racing, he didn't sit around and worry; he planned, strategized, and made it work. Martin is just one man, but I think American society could learn a thing or two from him. He was out of full-time racing for a while, but after careful planning and preparation, he was able to come back stronger than he ever was before. He didn't pity himself or wait for somebody to take care of him – he knew he'd probably need a sponsor to start racing again, but only he could put himself back on his feet. The moral of the story: you can't sit back and wait for somebody else to take care of you. You have to stay on top of what's going on in the world, figure out where you want to go, and get behind the wheel.

When the bills pour in, life gets stressful, and you just need to get away from it all. Sometimes the only place you want to go to is the races. NASCAR fans, no matter the level of the Dow on Wall Street or the number of bills in their mailbox, will find a way to get to the races. That ticket is more than money – it's a tradition, a spectacular event, a time to connect to a community. All they want is to see good racing. They want to hear the anthem and see America's finest vehicles out on the track.

Some people miss the old cars. The new cars, the stylish track, and the other technological advancements may add to the races, but they aren't the heart of the sport. Even if the economy reduced NASCAR to an old dirt track, used cars, and guys in dirty T-shirts, sunglasses, and jeans, the sport would go on. Fans would keep coming. NASCAR would be changed, but not necessarily for the worse. It's a down-to-earth sport, and it doesn't need the latest technological advancements to survive. That's not what the sport started as, and that's not what it necessarily needs to keep going. It's not about the technology, engineering, or even how fast you can go; it's about the community and the spirit of the sport.

With the cost of the cars, tracks, fuel, and repairs, NASCAR is one of the most expensive sports. Still, getting those cars on the track isn't just about racing. Those vehicles represent American business and innovation. They show what our car companies and engineers are capable of producing. The automobile is a vital part of American culture. Just like your job is a part of your identity, your car represents who you are and what you can accomplish. NASCAR represents, on a larger scale, the advancements in automobile engineering and the economic fortitude upon which that this country was built and will prevail.

At a time when many hard-working Americans couldn't afford health care and people were losing their jobs every day without a way to support themselves or their families, the government was sending tax dollars to large auto corporations. Yet Ford, one of the greatest American automakers of today and yesterday, refused bail-out money. There's something very American about a company that pulls itself up by the boot straps, tightens its belt, and says, no, that money can go toward people who need it.

When you hear about a formidable business like Ford turning down money and rightfully redirecting it to better causes, it makes you proud to be American. It's important that those cars and automakers keep racing down NASCAR's tracks. That might mean a few changes in the sport and limited testing. But even if those changes take a bit of the edge off of NASCAR, the spirit of the sport will endure. Even if the economy washed away all of the new gizmos that have made NASCAR's vehicles so aerodynamically capable that they can nearly fly . . . even if NASCAR's tracks were reduced to rubble due to lack of maintenance funds and the drivers were racing on dirt roads . . . even if we were broadcasting with a hand-held camera . . . NASCAR would still stay strong.

Over sixty years ago, down South, two rebels sat behind the wheels of average American vehicles with trunks full of moonshine on an old back road. They asked themselves how fast they could go. They didn't have money, sponsors, or engineers. All they needed was four wheels, moonshine, and a passion for racing. People started watching those daredevils as they raced head to head, never imagining that it would someday turn into the sport that fueled a nation. But that's exactly what happened. That fiery love of racing became an American passion.

It's never stopped since.

12

VICTORY

America is the greatest country on earth. It's a country where, no matter your status or background, you have the right to pursue your dreams, to speak your mind freely, to care for your family, and offer your children the brightest and fairest future possible. It's a country where potential is boundless, where hard work, dedication, and integrity go rewarded. So it's no small wonder that America is the birthplace of NASCAR.

NASCAR is at its core an American sport, a sport defined by American values, American sense of risk and reward, and an American thirst for speed, competition, and achievement. America is a nation of risk takers. We recognize that you can't change the status quo by hiding from possibility, and so we're a nation of people willing to go out on a limb, to take a chance, whether the outcome we're seeking is a more secure future for our children or just a thrilling weekend afternoon. After all, our forefathers instilled in us the power and potential of a little risk. Where would we be if they had decided to sit at home safe and pay taxes instead of taking the risk of speaking out and eventually arming themselves against the British crown?

That tradition has defined the progress of our nation ever since – from Abraham Lincoln risking political popularity for the cause of equality to Henry Ford risking his financial livelihood for the sake of an innovative product that would revolutionize the lives of generations of Americans to come. We know that no gain comes without risk, and we also know that a little healthy risk is just plain fun. America is a place where people can achieve more than they ever thought possible – and it's because we've got the courage to test our physical, emotional, financial, and personal limits. That same spirit is embodied on every NASCAR track in the country. There is no car race without risk – and there is no winner without risk.

America is a land of pride. We honor the heroes who gave us our freedom generations ago, who have defended that freedom over the centuries, and who continue to stand for it today. We are the freest country in the world, a country where the potential of the individual to better himself is celebrated and supported. We're willing to fight for that freedom, and we're willing to stand proud for it. This is our home, the place where we raise our children to bright futures and grow old knowing we've lived well.

In this country, patriotism isn't about posturing; it isn't a performance for the benefit of the cameras. It's something that every citizen feels deeply and expresses spontaneously, and nowhere is that expression more evident than at a NASCAR race track, in the solemnity of the fans standing for the anthem, in the honor the drivers and crew members pay to members of the military, and in the common goal to achieve as much as possible – for the sake of our country.

Americans know how to have fun. We live in one of the biggest countries in the world, where the open road stretches from sea to shining sea. The highway and the automobile are part of our way of life; they represent our freedom and spontaneity. And speed is the essence of the car culture. When we work, we keep busy, we accomplish things, we move from one goal to the next. And when we play, we play hard – we take risks, we watch exciting sports, we drive fast.

NASCAR is nothing if not the celebration of speed. It's the thrill of rubber on asphalt, the nose-to-nose excitement, the adrenaline, the glory. Americans love speed. And speed is what NASCAR is all about.

Our country is built on the labor of teams. We're proud to lend a hand to pull a fellow American up behind us. Sure, we're independent, but from the beginning, we've always known that if you want to reach greatness, you can't go it alone. From the cooperation in our businesses to the smoothness with which our servicemen and women depend on one another to defend the country, we know how to work together, and that's how we achieve high goals that we could never accomplish alone. A NASCAR driver is the face of the team, but it's the whole unit of ownership, sponsors, and crew that makes him great. It would be impossible to win a race – or even finish a race – alone, and when a driver crosses the finish line in first place, the glory belongs with the whole team, just as any one American's victory is a victory for all Americans.

America is a country of industry, a country of healthy competition, and a country where we value hard work enough to reward it. We know better than to judge a person's worth by the size of their car, their house, or their paycheck, but we also appreciate the healthy competition inherent in a capitalist system. At the same time we're practical enough to realize that while the American dream means anyone can achieve their potential, some people face financial limitations and challenges, while others might have an easier path. NASCAR is an expensive sport, and in some ways that limits access. But it still celebrates the independent drivers who take a chance with the big guys, and it welcomes hard-working, regular people into the stands more so than any other sport. NASCAR rewards the success of its teams – but drivers, owners, and crew members alike are out there for the love of the race, not for the money.

We've always been at the forefront of the world's technological breakthroughs. This country is one that values progress, innovation, and great products that make people's lives safer, easier, more efficient, or more comfortable. We're always pushing the envelope, testing limits, and when we see a problem or a challenge, we find ways to solve it with new ideas. NASCAR is, of course, a sport that depends on cutting-edge technology. Teams are under tremendous pressure to have superb, well-maintained machines at the forefront of the industry. And because there's a certain amount of danger inherent in the sport, NASCAR has adapted technology to constantly improve upon the safety of the drivers. This is a sport where innovation is celebrated – and where good ideas often spread outward to improve the lives of the everyday consumer.

For Americans, family comes first. We value passing on the heritage of our ancestors to our children, and above all else, we strive to give our children the most opportunities possible. We celebrate the traditions that have made us unique – made us Americans – over centuries, and it's crucial to us to keep incorporating those traditional values in our lives today. At the same time, we recognize the necessity of welcoming progress and new perspectives. We're the most open land in the world, where new cultures are constantly being woven into our own. And it's exactly the same in the NASCAR world. The sport was founded on strong traditions, born in the U.S.A. and built from grassroots, but NASCAR also recognizes that to thrive – and even just to survive – it can't be closed off. It's constantly looking for new venues and new audiences, while never losing touch with the original traditions that made it great to begin with.

America is a big country, and its people love bigness. We eat big burgers, we drive big cars, and in many ways, we're larger than life. It's not about being pushy or showy; it's just one more way of reflecting the enormous and sincere pride we feel in our country and our way of life. That's why NASCAR has huge tracks that seat tens of thousands of fans, so that everyone is welcome to take part in the excitement and pride of the race. That's why the cars are beautiful and gleaming – because it's important to teams that the precision and performance of the engines be reflected on the outside, not hidden and minimized. That's why every race has an air of fanfare and the national anthem is played to a thunderous cheer from the crowd. The pageantry of NASCAR reflects the heartfelt pride we all feel in the sport and in being fellow Americans. It's a way of showing the world how exciting it is to achieve greatness.

Americans teach their children to honor the heroes who won their freedom. I'm not just talking about heroes like George Washington, but also the everyday men and women who took up arms or built homesteads or founded businesses and schools. We value gratitude and honoring the sacrifice of our fellow Americans, who work and fight to keep our country great. On the NASCAR track, there are heroes of the sport, men who win race after race, or men who pull themselves up by their bootstraps, underdogs who in the last lap nose ahead to take the glory of the win. Sure, we applaud these heroes, and we're happy that our children look to them as role models. But NASCAR is also a sport for everyday people. The men and women in the stands are honored for their hard work and rewarded with an exciting event, a time when they can relax and get lost in the adrenaline and thrill of the race. The true heroes of America are its working people, its backbone – and NASCAR honors that.

And last – but certainly not least – America is a country of survivors. We've experienced glorious highs and mind-boggling progress alongside tragic wars and weakened economies, and through it all, we remain proud, strong, enduring. NASCAR is, in the most obvious sense, a sport about endurance. Where else do athletes travel hundreds of miles in one race, through high temperatures and extreme pressure, even through crashes? But it's not just on the track that endurance is key. It's also the sport itself that endures – that builds on its foundations and continues to find new ways to reach people, new markets to crack, and new ways to grow. It's that sense of never settling that makes America great and that will keep NASCAR at the forefront of the sports industry for years to come.

The future is bright. I see many opportunities for NASCAR to continue to grow in the years ahead. Already, NASCAR has started to stretch not just toward the northern part of the United States and to cities on the coasts, but also internationally. NASCAR has established the NASCAR Canadian Tire Series that runs solely in Canada, and the NASCAR Mexico Series that runs solely in Mexico. It's easier for NASCAR to reach other countries in North America just because of the practical concern of land transport – getting the cars from one track to the other. But NASCAR has now extended its reach to European soil, and in 2012, NASCAR is sanctioning a series overseas.

The American lifestyle is still a coveted idea, a way of being, overseas. It's not just the sport of NASCAR that I've seen people in England and other parts of Europe get excited about. It's the ruggedness of the sport and the sense of freedom and possibility that comes with fast cars and open road. They have rich racing traditions, to be sure, but they don't spend their weekends under the hoods of their cars, tinkering and making them faster the way we Americans do. We're still the Wild West in a lot of ways, and our car represents more than mobility. It represents freedom. It might be that NASCAR will never hold the same symbolism and importance there as it does here. But there is huge potential in the European market, and NASCAR sees the new avenues they can explore there. They are proud to be partnering up with European countries to start a 2012 racing series.

As we are slowly pulling ourselves out of the troubled economy and picking up our scattered pieces, NASCAR has also had to figure out a future plan. Maybe international venues or different kinds of sponsorship are two ways of doing that. Another way is just to tighten the belt temporarily, as so many of us are doing in our individual lives. Maybe instead of a new 100,000-seat venue, we'll be looking at a 65,000-seat one. There could be further adjustments and corrections in the number of races or in the ticket pricing. NASCAR and the tracks hosting events have to keep selling out races, continue to keep that excitement and buzz going, and if that's not possible when you've got 100,000-seat venues and ticket prices where they currently are, adjustments will be made.

As I discussed, NASCAR is all about endurance. And although we all saw the past collapse of the auto industry, there have still been plenty of opportunities within NASCAR. There continues to be a great feeling of optimism in the industry – even while everyone stays in touch with reality and pays closer attention to what is actually happening in the country. Baseball, another tried-and-true American sport, survived through wars and the Depression and an almost-devastating labor dispute. In 2011, the NBA experienced labor disputes and for the first time since 1999, owners imposed a lockout, creating a work stoppage. By the time negotiations were completed, the season had been truncated to a sixty-six game season as opposed to eighty-two, but even this did not deter the fans or the players from picking up their jerseys and posting up, either on the courts or in the stands. Football is another survivor, the gold standard. They have revenue sharing throughout the ownership, a commissioner who's in charge and maintains the real power, and a players' union that isn't stronger than the actual ownership of the sport. They listen to and talk to fans and use technology to their advantage – they're the birthplace of the instant replay, which totally revolutionized televised sports. They get through things, good and bad. And NASCAR has that same spirit.

People live for race day, it gets them through the week, and NASCAR isn't going to disappoint. Over the last century, the development of racing has tied in with the growth of the automobile in America. It used to be that a car was a luxury; it was rare to have one. If you did, it was just a seat and an engine; you didn't even have a seat belt. Now almost everyone has a car, and it's like a second home. You have a navigation system, Bluetooth, a DVD player in the back for the kids. When you think of how essential the car is in our daily lives – most of our livelihoods depend on having a way to get to and from work – it's plain as day that the car culture is here to stay. And if it is, so is NASCAR.

NASCAR will make whatever adjustments it needs to stay around, because it's that much a part of America. Whatever we've been through with the auto industry and the national economy, the sport is strong. NASCAR's future is firmly tied to America's future. And in a country with such strong values and clear vision, the future is bright. NASCAR is America. Freedom and speed are our birthright. The urge to compete and be the best is in our blood. Is the pursuit of happiness best illustrated by the Chase for the NASCAR Sprint Cup? After a decade covering NASCAR, I'd have to say, "Yes." Wouldn't you?

INDEX